PRAISE FOR
HEAVY TRAFFIC

Heavy Traffic is an honest account of the very real problem of sex trafficking. I was honored to spend over a decade under the leadership of Mel and Twyla Baggett on street outreach. The experience, at times, caused compassion fatigue and vicarious traumatization for those of us serving alongside the Baggetts, but with God as our guide, we ministered to the needs of those enslaved in human trafficking.

These accounts are true. I am a licensed mental health clinician who, more than twenty-five years ago, experienced the horror of the streets myself. I believe that this truth needs to be revealed: Human trafficking is modern-day slavery and is happening in our neighborhoods.

I celebrate that *Heavy Traffic* is giving a voice to those enslaved in sex trafficking so that freedom in Christ can become a reality for more people. Mel and Twyla Baggett made a difference in the lives of many enslaved on the streets of Metro Detroit. My hope is that this book helps others to do the same by bringing awareness to what is happening in our country today.

—Veronica H. Lopiccolo, MA, LPC, NCC, ACS, CCTP
All Things Possible Wellness Centers

HEAVY TRAFFIC

A WALK OF FAITH THROUGH THE EVIL OF SEX TRAFFICKING

Founders of Night Angels Detroit

MEL & TWYLA BAGGETT

Heavy Traffic
© 2025 by Mel and Twyla Baggett

This book is available at special discounts when purchased in quantity for use as premiums, promotions, fundraisers, or for educational purposes. For inquiries and details, contact the author at twylabaggett@yahoo.com.

Published by Courageous Heart Press
College Station, Texas

Editing and Design by My Writers' Connection

Library of Congress Control Number: 2024926550
Paperback ISBN: 978-1-950714-47-6
Ebook ISBN: 978-1-950714-48-3

Scriptures are taken from the NEW INTERNATIONAL VERSION (NIV): Scripture taken from THE HOLY BIBLE, NEW INTERNATIONAL VERSION ®. Copyright© 1973, 1978, 1984, 2011 by Biblica, Inc.™. Used by permission of Zondervan.

GET HELP NOW

If you need help or suspect that someone is in
imminent danger or is being trafficked,
call 911 to report it.

You can also call the
National Human Trafficking Hotline at
(888) 373-7888 for assistance.

CONTENTS

THE INVISIBLE CRIME THAT HAPPENS *EVERYWHERE*

human trafficking (noun): organized criminal activity in which human beings are treated as possessions to be controlled and exploited (as by being forced into sex work or involuntary labor)[1]

Human trafficking happens everywhere. Chances are good, in fact, that it's happening right now in your hometown.

With estimated global profits of $150 billion, human trafficking is one of the largest criminal enterprises in the world—ranking in the top three alongside illegal drug and arms trafficking.[2] The statistics surrounding human trafficking are all *estimated*, with the numbers varying widely from one agency or organization to the next. In 2021, the US State Department estimated that 27.6 million men, women, and children are caught in human trafficking worldwide. We believe, however, that the real number of victims is likely double that. Most experts won't try to project an actual number of slaves in the United States, but we believe it is in the millions. What we do know is that reported crimes reveal 80 percent of slaves are females, and 50 percent are children.

Why do the numbers vary so widely? Some of the reasons are obvious. For one, criminals don't register their illegal businesses down at the courthouse. The US Departments of Justice and Homeland Security report thousands of arrests each year, but we know that for every trafficker who is apprehended, many more are still at work victimizing people.

Additionally, multiple victims are involved in almost every reported case; for example, the National Human Trafficking Hotline identified 9,619 cases in 2023, in which 16,999 victims were involved.[3] Reported cases reveal only a fraction of the real numbers.

And finally, most victims of human trafficking are too afraid to report or ask for help, even if they have the opportunity to do so. Others do not realize or believe they are being trafficked, so even if they have an opportunity to tell someone, they don't.

While it is difficult to say exactly how many people are being trafficked worldwide or even here in the United States, what we can say with certainty is that **human trafficking is modern-day slavery.** The crime is often categorized in two ways:

- **Forced labor**, which can include domestic servitude, commercial labor, or child labor.
- **Sex trafficking**, a form of forced labor in which victims are coerced or involuntarily involved in commercial sex acts that can include prostitution, escort services, strip clubs, pornography, and forced marriages.

Human trafficking is often called an invisible crime. In small towns and big cities across the nation, victims are coerced or forced to live as slaves—and most of the time, no one notices them or the pain and danger they are in. That is certainly true where we live in Detroit, where the infrastructure that was developed to support the automobile industry decades ago makes it easy and efficient for modern-day slave traders from across the United States and around the world to move people in and out of the city. The I-75 corridor moves victims north and south, while the Ohio Turnpike helps to move them east and west throughout the country. Geography, both our proximity to Canada and the waterways adjacent to the Great Lakes that surround the state, also assists traffickers in carrying out their heinous acts. Slaves get shipped into the United States from Canada and Eastern Europe through our tunnels and bridges and across the beautiful Great Lakes.

HOW WE GOT HERE

We want to take a few paragraphs to introduce ourselves, not because we're *special* but because we hope that, somewhere in our story, you may see yourself and your potential to impact others' lives with the love of Jesus wherever you live.

We, the authors of this book, are Mel and Twyla Baggett, and we raised our family in a suburb of Detroit, Michigan, a city that is a hub for human trafficking. Of course, we didn't know that when we decided to build our lives here. It wasn't until much later that we learned about the depravity that happens every day in Detroit and realized God was calling us to do something about it. We had come to love this city and its people.

Actually, Mel has loved Detroit since he was a child growing up in one of the city's blue-collar neighborhoods. He attended Detroit public schools from elementary school all the way through high school graduation and went on to college at Detroit's Wayne State University. Mel's dad worked for the Detroit Free Press, one of the city's major daily newspapers. The office was in the downtown area, so from an early age, Mel learned to love the hustle and bustle of city life. He still can't imagine having grown up anywhere else.

Twyla, on the other hand, lived most of her childhood in a one-stop-light town in Northwest Indiana. Her younger years, filled with dance lessons, bike rides, and small-town traditions, were quite different from Mel's. Life changed dramatically for Twyla when her father took a job with an automotive parts manufacturer and supplier in Detroit. Her family moved to their new suburban home just before what became known as the "long, hot summer of 1967." That was the summer that more than 150 riots ripped apart cities across the United States. One of the bloodiest of those urban riots occurred that July in Detroit. The intense fear Twyla and her family experienced that summer stayed with her for years, tainting the way she felt about the city. At home, Twyla experienced a different kind of fear brought on by emotional, physical, and sexual abuse at the hands of the people who should have protected and loved her.

From the outside, Twyla's family appeared to be the perfect model for the American dream. They had a beautiful home in an upper-class suburban neighborhood, fancy cars, and a summer cottage in Northern Michigan. Twyla's home life, though, left much to be desired. Her beautiful mother could have been an understudy for Elizabeth Taylor, but that beauty was only skin deep. The ugliness beneath surfaced daily as she lashed out at Twyla verbally, emotionally, and physically. Twyla's father, an imposing six foot, two inch man, had a presence that rivaled the Marlboro man. He fooled everyone with his small-town charm, but the truth was he lacked the capacity for love and empathy. Behind closed doors, he used his strength and size against his daughter. Throughout her childhood and adolescence, he would force her to undress before whipping her. The emotional and physical scars from the treatment she endured as a young girl remain with Twyla to this day. They also gave her a powerful sense of empathy for those suffering as victims of abuse and injustice.

We met as teenagers during a Christian youth conference in Ann Arbor, Michigan, in 1970. We had no way of knowing back then what God would do with our lives and, honestly, had no expectation that we would ever find our ways into ministry or mission work. Looking back, however, we know God was putting the pieces into place when He brought together two teenagers from opposite sides of Detroit. What started as friendship led to flirting, eventually becoming a union of two people who would cling to, laugh with, and love each other for the rest of their lives.

Things weren't smooth or easy after that initial meeting, though. Twyla's parents wouldn't allow her to date. We lived on opposite sides of town and didn't have our own cars, so we relied on friends for transportation when we wanted to see each other. Mel started attending the same church as Twyla, which made Sundays one of our favorite days.

As soon as it became clear to us that marriage was in our future, we started planning for our life together. Even before we were engaged, we put furniture on layaway. Each week we held hands as we walked to the store to pay another five dollars toward our dream.

We got married soon after Twyla graduated from high school. Mel had just finished his second year of college. Plenty of people told us that our teenage marriage wouldn't last. *Who were we to think we could beat the odds?* Certainly, time has proved that married life can be difficult, even when you're with someone who deeply loves you. But for Twyla, marriage was a way out of an untenable life of ugly abuse. So pooling our money, we paid for a simple wedding with a cake-and-punch reception at the church we attended. Fifty years later (and counting), Twyla still calls Mel her "knight in shining armor."

We started our new, peaceful life in a little rented apartment in Detroit on Eight Mile Road and Lahser. (Yes, there really is an Eight

Mile Road in Detroit). Things grew continually busier as our studies, careers, and, later, our family expanded. When we got married, Mel was studying criminal justice and planned to become a Detroit police officer, a job that, at the time, required applicants to live within the city's limits. He later shifted tracks and built a long career in human resources with the Ford Motor Company. Before he retired from his position as vice president of human resources in 2013, he had seen the company morph from a small division into a 10-billion-dollar steel-making giant with operations across North America.

Twyla became a legal assistant in a prestigious law firm in Birmingham, Michigan, and worked there until our two daughters came along. Looking for a little more flexibility, Twyla shifted her career path and became a paraprofessional teacher at a local Christian school where she stayed for seventeen years. Raising two wonderful daughters is what Twyla is most proud of. And now, being a grandmother is what she refers to as the "cherry topping" on her cake.

We drifted away from church in our early years of marriage. Despite our rebellion that was rooted in apathy and the pursuit of worldly success, we remained aware of God's presence and His call for us to know Him. On our tenth wedding anniversary, December 4, 1984, we recommitted our lives to Christ. From that day on, the Lord seemed to put our lives into hyper-gear as we learned more about Him and grew to love Him more.

In the years that followed, we remained active in our church community. Upon approaching the time of Mel's retirement, however, we assessed the state of our faith. We had performed virtually every job within the four walls of our church—from changing diapers in the nursery, teaching Sunday school classes for toddlers, raising funds, teaching catechism, and serving as deacons, elders, and even a trustee of the church. The one church activity we hadn't done was to go on a mission trip. Work had always prevented Mel from taking off the necessary time.

TAKING OUR FAITH OUTSIDE THE CHURCH WALLS

In our new stage of life, we envisioned going to the jungles of Africa or the mountains of Mexico—possibly the coastlines of Thailand, China, or Central America. We wanted to test and hopefully prove and strengthen our faith. For years, we had prayed for and ministered to people where it was easy: in Sunday school classes, during times of worship, and at the altar. The question we wanted to answer for ourselves was, did we have the backbone to put our faith to work outside the protection of a church building?

Did we have the backbone to put our faith to work outside the protection of a church building?

As we researched and considered several opportunities in the mission field, we learned about the problem of human trafficking. It seemed impossible, at first. *Slavery in our world today?* Then we assumed that *if* human trafficking existed, it only happened in faraway places like Thailand, Vietnam, Eastern Europe, or maybe China. But not the United States, where Abraham Lincoln's signing of the Emancipation Proclamation had abolished slavery so long ago. Surely, slavery couldn't still exist in the United States today. Right?

Wrong.

What we learned is that it exists everywhere. Yes, even in our beloved hometown of Detroit. The realization caused a swell of righteous indignation to rise up in both of us.

The city had come so far since the late 1960s. It was finally flourishing with the help and leadership of good people like Mike and Marian Ilitch, Dan Gilbert, and many others who worked hard to ensure Detroit's people could thrive. We struggled to wrap our minds around the fact that, despite all the good happening in the city, the evil of human trafficking could be hiding in the smokestacks, alleyways, and side streets.

The more we learned, the more we realized the magnitude of the problem. We knew that God was calling us to get involved. Our mission field wasn't on another continent or in a developing country; it was just a few miles from our suburban home, and coincidentally, right down the street from our first apartment.

NIGHT ANGELS TAKE FLIGHT

We volunteered with a Christian-based anti-trafficking group for well over two years before forming a 501(c)(3) nonprofit called Night Angels in 2016. Our Night Angels team members came from a cross-section of Christian denominations and churches. None were pastors or highly educated theologians. They were simply people with regular jobs and lives who loved God and had a desire to serve. These men and women served as outreach members, drivers, prayer warriors, trackers, mentors, administrative assistants, advisers, speakers, media specialists, and inventory managers. They had heard about the problem of trafficking and were incensed at the injustice.

Our life experiences, including Mel's work in human resources and Twyla's childhood abuse and teaching role, had given us empathy toward people who were hurting or in challenging situations. But we weren't academically prepared for the work set before us. We didn't have experience in psychology, psychiatry, or social work.

God filled the gaps in our experience by appointing Angels to the ministry from every walk of life. Nurses, therapists, teachers, homemakers, a chef, an actress, a writer, a farmer, an accountant, a Navy Seal, and others joined our team. Imbued with the power of the Holy Spirit, they volunteered to be the boots on the ground in a war that the devil seems to be winning by stealing the hearts and lives of our family members every day. Each person on the team, including the two of us, willingly offered their time and energy and heart. No one received a paycheck.

Jeremiah 29:11 served as our biblical cornerstone:

> *"For I know the plans I have for you," declares the Lord,*
> *"plans to prosper you and not to harm you, plans to give you*
> *hope and a future."*

We developed an operating plan to tactically lay out how we would pursue our ministry activities in this fight. We referred to them as the Four A's:

Awareness

To raise awareness about the problem of trafficking, we have spoken to Sunday school classes, Brownie troops, and Bible study groups, as well as at police departments, church meetings, high schools, and fraternal organizations. We have spoken on television and radio, debated with panelists in various venues, and met with representatives at the Michigan Capitol to encourage changing the laws in our state. Training at colleges and universities became routine for us when awareness education was made mandatory for professionals.

Part of awareness included making people aware of the risks and the signs of trafficking. Another element was raising awareness of the realities. We start by dispelling myths and misconceptions, like the *Pretty Woman* fallacy. First, no woman chooses to become a prostitute. She ends up there because she has become vulnerable. The women and men working on the streets did not choose that life. They are almost always controlled by a trafficker. The trafficker can be a parent, husband, drug dealer, pimp, or madame. Many traffickers don't look like how you might expect. Some have respectable jobs and fit in with everyday society. But they are traffickers or controllers just the same.

No woman chooses to become a prostitute. She ends up there because she has become vulnerable.

The second part of the *Pretty Woman* fallacy is that sex-trafficked women look nothing like "Vivian," the beautiful character Julia Roberts portrays in the 1990 film. Most are between twelve and sixty-five years old. They are emaciated, usually weighing between seventy-five and ninety pounds. Most are missing several (if not all) of their teeth and are in poor health. They will often go weeks or longer between showers and are covered in bug bites, needle marks, abscessed infections caused by using dirty needles, prison tattoos, and sometimes gang markings. Their dirty, unbrushed hair is thinning from malnutrition.

Often, sex-trafficking victims are addicted to illegal drugs, which they are put on against their will. The addiction ensures they will return for their next fix so that the trafficker doesn't have to use chains, whips, or handcuffs to enslave them.

They are sporting bruises, bloody lips, and knife punctures from the violent "dates" they survived while trying to make the quota that their trafficker has given them for the day. Many girls stay awake for multiple days in a row trying to earn their quota. If they don't make their quota, they are beaten, abused, punished, or even killed. They do not live in homes. They might get to lay their weary body down on the bare floor of a crack house *if* they can bring in an extra ten dollars. The house would be without heat, electricity, water, windows, furniture, or even a toilet.

All the money they make belongs to the trafficker. Aside from the clothes that they're wearing, they carry everything they own in a small purse or backpack.

There is nothing *pretty* about this life.

Assistance

Many anti-human trafficking organizations speak to awareness, but few do actual street outreach. This is what our team became known for. Night Angels went out in a four-person team in an SUV with at least an additional two members at home watching and praying for our evening outreach.

We would drive around looking for people we believed were engaged in sex work. Experience taught us that sex workers are usually sex-trafficking victims. When we pulled up in the SUV, we'd offer a free lunch and a hygiene kit to the person. The first meeting was often met with rejection. A typical response was, "Screw you"; however, when we showed up faithfully at the same time and place every week, our friends on the street warmed up to us. As soon as the ice was broken, we wanted to bring Jesus Christ into the dynamic. We would ask them first if we could pray with them. It was through the prayer requests that we truly began to know about them, their families, and their troubles, as well as the streets and conditions of their environment. The prayer, lunch, and hygiene kit were intended to build trust with the trafficking victim whom we called our friend.

We wanted our friends to trust us enough to let us help them get away from their traffickers and the chaos in which they were living. At each encounter, we left a business card with our hotline number where they could reach one of us 24/7.

Then we hoped and prayed they would dial the number and reach out to us for help.

When those calls for help came in, our team began the rescue. The most immediate issue is always safety—how to safely get them away from their trafficker and the environment in which they have been living. The next issue to deal with is addiction, as almost all our friends had a variety of addictions. Usually, it was heroin, with secondary addictions to crack cocaine, alcohol, meth, and various other substances. The illicit use of fentanyl caused a wave of deaths that surged between 2011 and 2018 and is once again rising. We would try to get our friends into detox and then long-term drug treatment programs by offering to help them use the social system to get the help they needed. There are a number of good programs here in Southeastern Michigan. Grace Centers of Hope, a Christ-centered private facility in Pontiac, Michigan, was always our first choice; unfortunately, demand for their services is high, and space isn't always available.

Advocacy

Getting people to safety and into detox and drug rehab were just the first steps. As friends, we wanted to stay in touch and help them where we could. Recognizing our limitations (we weren't social workers or psychologists), we connected them with the social services they needed to help them long-term: legal assistance, recreating personal documents, securing health services, and finding a church. We continued in a relationship of mentoring and encouragement with our survivors for as long as they wanted us to be with them. Many of them have grown to be much more than survivors of human trafficking. They are thriving in our community.

Apostleship

Our model for this type of outreach worked to help free people from physical slavery. In some cases, our friends also came to know the freedom of Christ. Our desire was and is to help others begin a work like Night Angels in communities around the world. With this mission in mind, we have talked with other mission-minded people as far away as London, England and as close as the thumb in Michigan. By encouraging and training others and by sharing our recipe for a successful outreach program with many organizations, we hope and pray this work continues until every trafficked person is free.

MAKING THE INVISIBLE VISIBLE

In the ten-plus years of ministry on our local mission field, our Christ-centered team of Angels was privileged to meet, feed, clothe, and pray for more than 7,000 victims of sex trafficking in just three areas of the city of Detroit. It was our honor to be chosen to share the love of Christ with each of them. The Lord used the Night Angels team to rescue more than 600 of His children from the streets. *To God be all the glory!*

In 2023, we closed the nonprofit ministry we had created. After ten years, we felt that God was leading us to share these stories and raise a call for awareness beyond the boundaries of Detroit. Although we have retired from our Night Angels ministry, we can't simply walk away from the people who so desperately need help. With this book, our mission of awareness continues. Our hope is that by reading the stories of the women and men we encountered, you will be moved into action in your community. Our story proves that you don't have to travel around the world to serve God in mighty ways. Opportunities wait for you on the street corners, at the downtown motel, and in broken lives in communities and every city of this nation.

Our hope is that by reading the stories of the women and men we encountered, you will be moved into action in your community.

This book shares stories about just a few of the people we were blessed to get to know through our ministry. We love each one of these people and respect their privacy and their pain. With that in mind, we have changed the names and all identifying details to ensure they will not be recognized or retraumatized by our writing. Some stories are composites and some required that we fill in a few gaps that the person either didn't recall or was too traumatized to tell. These changes are simply to ensure that the stories are cohesive, not to dramatize or exaggerate the reality of the streets and the world of sex trafficking. It is impossible for us to fully describe the ugliness of the evil these victims and our team members witnessed; there is simply no need to exaggerate or dramatize the truth.

As we tell the stories of our beloved friends from the street, we hope that you will see them for who they are: real people who have endured tremendous pain and suffering. What they've shared with us and what we've experienced with them will give you a glimpse into their feelings and the reality of their lives.

You'll read about the cumulative effects of trafficking. After reading these stories, you will never again say that prostitution is a victimless crime or that viewing pornography doesn't hurt anyone.

You'll also have a better understanding of how a person becomes vulnerable to this crime and how traffickers spot and use the person's vulnerability to gain control over them.

Some will say, "These stories can't be true." Others will say, "This can't be reality."

We understand. Disbelief and denial were our initial reactions, too, when we first learned about human trafficking. Yet after ten years of witnessing the real-life effects of these horrors, we can assure you that human trafficking is real, and it is evil.

Our hope is that this book opens your eyes to see the people who are hurting in your own community. We pray it inspires you to step out in faith and become an angel to someone in need.

"For I know the plans I have for you," declares the LORD,
"plans to prosper you and not to harm you,
plans to give you hope and a future."
—Jeremiah 29:11

APRIL

It took many weeks of regular Monday night street outreach drives before our team began to fully understand the chaos in which our friends lived each day. The mayhem of the street was unlike anything any of us had seen or experienced in suburbia or even in the city. As we talked about and processed the individual elements together, a larger mosaic formed to give us a better picture of the culture on the street—how it looked and worked and how sinister it was.

But it wasn't just one thing that gave us the insight we had lacked going in. It was a collection of strange things—or things that were strange to us but absolutely ordinary to the street's tumultuous environment.

It was seeing Helga going potty on the sidewalk while sitting on a milk crate (blanket covering her bottom half).

It was meeting John (who seemed to be the mayor of the street in which we were working) walking and talking to everyone, collecting the latest gossip, and trying, with little means at his disposal, to help everyone he could.

It was meeting "The Teacher," who had gathered a group of individuals who were living in tents they had pitched in an alley about a block off the main road.

It was seeing those people being run off by the police when city authorities decided that the tent city, which could be seen by VIPs traveling from Metro Airport to downtown Detroit, wasn't good for Detroit's image.

It was watching the fentanyl that had been mixed into the heroin our friends injected turn their skin orange—and being unable to do anything about it.

It was witnessing one of our friends cut off her court-ordered electronic tether—and not trying to stop her because she was known to carry a gun in her purse.

It was seeing one of our friends taking a shower and shaving her legs in the spray car wash as we drove by. She smiled and waved at us as if what she was doing was completely normal. To her, it was.

It was the hundreds of times we saw our friends and the homeless from the neighborhood going dumpster diving for scraps of food.

It was when we saw a phone vendor trying to give away free mobile phones to our friends, using money from a federal grant. The laughable, yet sad, thing was the useless grant itself. Without proper identification credentials, which our friends don't possess, the phone company can't meet the grant criteria necessary to give the phones away.

It was seeing one of our friends having sex in an open field twenty feet from the street where our team was ministering that evening, clearly unconcerned about being watched or caught by police. That girl was April.

We had met and prayed with April many times and had gotten to know her well. The scene ripped at our hearts and brought so many questions and concerns to mind. The first of which was, *what could have driven April to think it was okay to have sex in public where children might see her or other predators could further assault her?*

We knew April had been using heroin, crack cocaine, and a variety of other drugs for a long time. Our team's affection for the girl led us to wonder whether her critical-thinking skills had been lost, damaged by her drug addiction or the pain from the trauma she suffered daily. Or was there something else?

We knew that life for us and the way we approached our ministry would never be the same.

Seeing April that night gave each of us a hypersensitivity to the chaos in which our friends lived. We had a new understanding of the chaos. The way we viewed the street changed that night, and we knew that life for us and the way we approached our ministry would never be the same.

PATH TO PROSTITUTION

When we first met April, she was in her early twenties and had been on the street for several years. The first drug she had tried was marijuana at age thirteen. At fourteen, she piggy-backed crack cocaine to her drug use. She began snorting heroin at age nineteen. Drug use is what led her ultimately to being homeless, but the odds were stacked against her from the beginning.

April's mother, whom she dearly loved, was an alcoholic. Her biological father had disappeared after he and April's mother divorced. Her mother remarried, but her stepfather, too, was an alcoholic. With both of her parents dealing with addiction, April didn't have a chance to lead a drug-free life. It may have well been this stepfather who initially introduced April to drug use before he died from alcoholism in his early fifties. We also suspect that he may have sexually molested her, although April never confirmed that. She had stepsisters and stepbrothers, but because they didn't live in her home, she had little interaction with them.

The one bit of light in her dysfunctional life came from Grandma, her maternal grandmother. The older woman played a large role in April's life and tried to give her some semblance of a normal childhood, which included taking April with her to church. The impact of that early exposure to the Lord, limited though it was, became obvious when April prayed for *us*—a real treat for our street team. We loved hearing the energy and life in her prayers. Grandma's influence was evident even after she died.

When we prayed with April, she often asked us to pray for the child she had given up for adoption when she was just thirteen. Her first brush with sex trafficking occurred just a few years later. She was overweight as a teenager and had trouble finding a job. She finally found one working in a private home where a man hired her to care for his wife, who was dying of cancer. April was to perform the basic aspects of nursing and care for the woman, administering medicine, bathing and feeding her, and doing some light housework. The job would have been a great fit for April, who had an inner kindness. She truly enjoyed caring for people.

Unfortunately, the man who hired April did not have that same kindness in his heart. He offered drugs as part of her pay for the nursing care and then introduced her to sex work. He would arrange for men to come into his home and have sex with April. He and April would split the money exchanged. This arrangement with this pseudo-pimp introduced April to sex work, making it seem like an acceptable means of financial gain. The experience led to a sex addiction that would dominate her life for many years to come.

In the neighborhood where we ministered, April came in search of drugs. She was groomed for sex work and was being controlled by a man who ran a bordello. By this time, her drug use had skyrocketed, robbing her of her appetite and causing her to drop weight. Having grown up feeling worthless, she was surprised by the amount of money she made for the trafficker—and for herself—with sex work. She often said things like, "I never thought my body could ever make so much money." Yes, her trafficker let her keep some of the money she earned at the bordello, which was quite unusual. She told us that she felt her body had become like an ATM machine, and she didn't want to shut it down, because it fueled her drug use. (Which is probably why her trafficker allowed her to have some of the money from her sex work.)

FEAR. PRISON. *HOPE.*

When the first bordello that she worked at was busted, she moved down the street to a second one. It was while she was at this second bordello that she was coerced to get into a car with a "date," who drove her to a rural area about fifty miles from the neighborhood. When she went into the man's house and saw dog cages that were big enough to fit a human, she freaked out. The man threatened to lock her up in one of the cages and keep her there if she "didn't act right."

After brutalizing April and having sex with her, the man fell asleep. April waited. When she felt sure he was in a deep sleep, she bolted for the door. She ran until she found a gas station a few miles away and used the pay phone to call our hotline. Our team quickly drove to the gas station and picked April up. On the drive back to the city, she told us of the violence that had been perpetrated against her that night. She felt certain that the man intended to put her in one of those cages and not take her back to the bordello—ever. April told us she "was sick and tired of being sick and tired." Our team got the feeling that she had begun to make the connection between drug addiction, living in the streets, and the traffickers who were destroying her health and well-being. Still, she wasn't ready to break away from her trafficker at the bordello and go in for drug treatment.

April did not choose to go to detox and drug rehab that night; instead, she went to county jail several times and served time for petty crimes such as loitering, solicitation of prostitution, and possession of drug paraphernalia. At twenty-six, she was arrested for breaking and entering. The charge was pled down to larceny, for which she served ten months in the Huron Valley State Prison. That ten-month period was the longest she had been sober since she had turned thirteen. While she was in prison, she got some help with her mental and physical health issues—issues she hadn't realized she had. She was diagnosed with chlamydia, pulmonary embolism, bipolar disorder, manic disorder, social anxiety, and primary insomnia. To cap off all her other problems, while she was hospitalized during her prison stay, she contracted MRSA, a serious type of staph infection that is resistant to antibiotics.

Upon her release from incarceration, she had nowhere to call home other than the bordello where she had worked. On our next neighborhood outreach, she confided that she had made the decision to trust us to help her. She finally wanted to get detox and long-term drug rehabilitation. Over the next eighteen months, she went to a detox center three times. The first time we dropped her off, she spent only three hours there before running for the door; finally, on the third visit to the center, she stuck to the detox and the drug rehabilitation process and began true progress toward sobriety.

SCARRED. SOBER. *SAVED.*

April has maintained her sobriety for more than five years as of this writing. She works hard every day, using the tips and strategies she learned during her drug rehab. She is gainfully employed in the healthcare field and continues to receive high accolades and promotions for her dedication and leadership. She now has a little girl and is in a relationship with the girl's father.

The most important aspect of her sobriety is that she has a relationship with the Lord. April gives God all the credit for her ability to stay sober and conduct her life with a measure of normalcy. If you were to meet April today, you would not believe she is the same person we saw having sex in that open field so many years ago when her mental illness was untreated and her addictions were out of control. The many demons she was fighting at the time left a void in her only the Lord could fill.

> The most important aspect
> of her sobriety is that she has a
> relationship with the Lord.

April's scars run deep. With the help of medication, her mental illness is under control. She knows that she continually walks the tightrope of sobriety and mental stability. Although she lives with the father of her little girl, April doesn't trust men due to how she had been beaten, bruised, and forever maimed. The men who were her controllers and traffickers are imprisoned now, but she knows that when they get out, some may seek retribution against her. Others may try to get her back into life on the streets. But her story gives her and us hope.

April is a hero to our team. She has battled valiantly and has found the truth in her relationship with the Lord.

We wish her grandmother could see her now.

The Spirit of the Sovereign LORD is on me, because the LORD has anointed me to proclaim good news to the poor. He has sent me to bind up the brokenhearted, to proclaim freedom for the captives and release from darkness for the prisoners.

—*Isaiah 61:1*

TAYLOR

In the bitter cold of late January, the streets of Detroit are dark. The blue glow from the streetlights adds to the darkness, both visually and spiritually. As we drove down the salt-covered streets on those nights, we were especially thankful for the Dodge Durango that kept our four-person team safe and warm inside.

The differences between the streets on which we ministered and the ones Mel knew as a child were stark. His childhood home in that blue-collar neighborhood was on a street lined with shingled or aluminum-sided, 900-square-foot bungalows. The lawns had been immaculately kept, and the trim on the houses always seemed to be freshly painted.

In the warmer months, people sat on their front porches and visited with neighbors. Even in the cold of winter, kids were always playing outside or walking up and down the streets to find their friends or some minor mischief to engage in. One of the big games for kids was grabbing onto the bumpers of slow-moving cars for a free ride down the icy streets. Detroit never plowed its side streets, so after it snowed, boys would catch hold of a car's bumper and slide on their feet for a couple hundred yards. The joy of a good slide was entertaining.

One of the areas in which we worked had once been a blue-collar neighborhood not far from Mel's. Forty-five years earlier, the nice, large two-story brick homes had been turned into flats that housed two families. But time had taken its toll, and the streets were different now. There was no landscaping to speak of except litter and broken bottles. Security bars covered the windows that hadn't been broken or boarded up. No one hung around outside, but we knew that the traffickers, drug dealers, and gangsters lurked in the darkness as they went about their evil work.

BROKEN

One particularly cold evening in late January early in our ministry, we noticed how few people were out. On any given night, we usually saw ten to forty sex workers during our two-hour outreach drive, but that night we had seen only a few; finally, we spotted a girl standing on a corner of the street wearing a heavy, light-colored parka, blue jeans, and athletic shoes. She wasn't wearing a scarf, but we could hardly see her face because she was using her hands to shield her cheeks from the arctic wind. Despite the fact that the streets were almost empty, she appeared to be waiting for a customer.

A man stood no more than three feet from her as she waited, a display of control which told us two things: the girl was probably new to the streets, and her trafficker viewed her as a valuable commodity. Sex workers with long-term drug addictions don't usually have their traffickers standing so close to them as they transact business; they aren't as much of a flight risk.

In situations like that, we opted not to pull over. Any attempt we might have made that evening to strike up a conversation with her would likely have angered the trafficker and put her and our team in further danger. So we kept driving. We knew that we would be out there every week, on the same day, and at the same time—and chances were good that we would see her again. We were right.

Week after week, we saw the girl positioned on the street, and each week, her trafficker stood a little farther away from her. As his distance from her increased, we were able to get closer. We regularly offered her lunch and hygiene supplies and learned that her name was Taylor. She was the first trafficking victim we had met that we suspected was a victim of child prostitution (under the age of eighteen), and she really tugged at all our hearts. We brought her blankets and clothing early on to help her stay warm. Some of the parents of our team members even brought her an electric heater and additional blankets, hoping to somehow ease the pain of her situation.

Eventually, she stood there alone. With the drug addiction as an effective fetter, her trafficker was confident Taylor would return to him for another hit of the toxic poison he dispensed. He knew she had been *broken*. Sex traffickers use force and violence to break their victims and make them prisoners who believe there is no way out. It's typically a combination of violence and addictive drugs that solidifies the trafficker's control of their victims. That was certainly true in Taylor's case.

A GOOD KID FROM A GOOD FAMILY

The more we were able to talk with her, the more she trusted us. As the weeks went by, and we learned more about her, the heartstrings of our team became tightened by every chapter of the story she shared. Taylor grew up in a happy home with good parents in an upper middle-class neighborhood of Troy, Michigan. She had attended Athens High School, where she earned a 3.5 grade point average. (We had lived in Troy for a number of years, and it wasn't lost on us that our daughters would have attended Athens High if they'd been in public school.)

Taylor was a student athlete and made the soccer team her freshman year; unfortunately, she was injured almost immediately. To aid in her recovery, the doctor prescribed an opiate-based pain killer to which she quickly became addicted. When her body healed from the injury, the addiction remained.

The withdrawal she experienced when her doctor stopped writing prescriptions for the opiate were unbearable. To cope, Taylor used her babysitting money to purchase opiates from the dealers who hung out in the parking lot of her high school. The pills were expensive for a high school kid, costing anywhere from twenty to fifty dollars per tablet, depending on supply and demand. Taylor's cash flow from babysitting couldn't support her habit, and it wasn't long before she burned through any savings she had.

Taylor's parents were not neglectful or oblivious. They loved and cared for her dearly. So when they noticed the signs of drug use, they didn't hide their heads in the sand or look the other way. Instead, they sought help. They talked with her high school guidance counselor when her grades began to slip. They reached out to their family doctor to get her drug tested to see what drug she was using; in fact, they did everything they could to help her, including convincing her to go to drug rehabilitation. While she was there, Taylor's parents spoke with the facility's counselors to try to understand Taylor's problem. They wanted back the sweet and innocent daughter that the drugs had stolen from them.

Taylor tried to get away from the opiate addiction, but in the two years that followed, the cycle of drug use, drug detox, and drug rehabilitation spun three times. After the third trip to drug rehabilitation, Taylor's parents were saddened, tired, and frustrated when Taylor relapsed again into addiction.

This time, though, Taylor had moved from opiates to heroin, first snorting it and then using it intravenously. It was a faster, cheaper high. On the street, she could get a deck (dose) of heroin for $10 compared to the $50 it cost for a dose of Vicodin. To buy the heroin, she had to leave her upscale suburban neighborhood in Troy and travel to the streets of Detroit. There she would purchase her heroin from a drug dealer who was a part of a gang that operated on the north side of the city. It was a tragic decision.

EVIL INTENTIONS

Taylor was young and beautiful. So when the gang leader saw her, he put a plan in place to exploit the vulnerability of her drug addiction—and her—to make more money for the gang.

The gang leader, "Tiny," offered Taylor the drugs she wanted for free, so she stayed and partied with the gang members for several days. During that time, Tiny amped up each dose effectively increasing her body's demand for the drug. When she finally came out of the fog of her protracted high, she realized she had been gang raped. Various members of the gang had taken turns with her, and she was bleeding profusely from the damage they had done. In pain, afraid, and hooked on heroin, Taylor believed Tiny when he told her that she was worthless and couldn't go home because her family wouldn't want her anymore. Plus, she needed the heroin which Tiny had in good supply.

Tiny had his minions put Taylor on the street as a sex worker. She was just seventeen.

That's when we saw Taylor on that bitter January night for the first time.

For four months, we saw Taylor almost every week. With food, essentials, and genuine care, we worked to build a relationship with her. Each time we saw her, we prayed that something would *click* and that she would allow us to help her get to detox and find a road back to her family and ultimately to Jesus.

Then, suddenly, she was gone.

We asked our other friends on the street if they had seen Taylor; did they know what had happened to her? We heard a variety of stories, some that might have been true, others that certainly were not. Working on the streets requires a level of street smarts. One of the lessons we learned early on was that we couldn't always (or ever) take things at face value or believe every story we heard. One of our team rules was not to believe anything we heard on the street the first or second time we heard it. If we heard the same story a third time, we gave it some credence. After several weeks of gathering and sifting through snippets of information, the real story about Taylor began to take shape.

Tiny had been arrested in a drug raid. He had been incarcerated, and his imprisonment was going to last for some time. With Tiny gone, another gang member took over. This new leader was a savvier businessman than Tiny and knew that Taylor's good looks and youth were worth more than what she was bringing in as a prostitute on the street. Using his connections in the pornography industry, he sold Taylor to a pornography production group.

Some people believe that pornography is no big deal. The reality is that the pornography industry is the biggest user of sex-trafficking victims. Every time someone accesses pornography online, they are enabling and facilitating sex trafficking. The youngest, most attractive victims are exploited in this world, and Taylor was one of them. Sold like a commodity, she was forced in front of the camera. She acted in videos and did live-camera work, which refers to a setup where viewers pay to watch a girl(s) or boy(s) in a closed setting, usually a hotel room or brothel, through internet video calls.

> Every time someone accesses
> pornography online, they are enabling
> and facilitating sex trafficking.

The problem for Taylor and the pornographers was her heroin addiction. The amount she was using had increased dramatically over the previous several months. The porn producers had to throttle back her usage because the drug was taking a toll on her looks; additionally, her sustained high made it difficult for them to handle her. Weaning her to a much lower level gave her a better image for the camera, which increased the profit they could make off her. After about a year in the world of porn, Taylor found a way to get her hands on more of the drug she craved. Her addiction raged again out of control. Unable to use her anymore, the pornographers sold Taylor back to the gang that had controlled her before.

At eighteen, Taylor was back on the streets, being controlled by the gang and shackled by her addiction. Our team saw her again one night, and she looked so much older than her eighteen years. Her body was covered with gang markings and tattoos. Her hair was dirty and cut shorter, and the natural blonde had been replaced with shades of brown and dark red. She had never looked that way before, and we almost didn't recognize her.

Just like the first time we saw her, Taylor's controller stood right next to her. Because of his presence, we had not planned to pull over. We never wanted to put a trafficking victim or our team at greater risk. But when she saw us and called us over, we stopped and visited with her for a while as she confirmed the terrible story we'd heard about her on the street.

Before we drove away, Taylor told us we probably wouldn't see her around again because the gang had her working in another part of the city most of the time. That ended up being the truth.

We didn't see Taylor again, but we would never forget her. That young girl, who reminded all of us so much of our daughters and nieces and granddaughters, inspired us to return to the streets week after week. Her family's story could have been ours. Her parents, who loved her and whom she clearly loved and admired, did everything they could to help Taylor break free from her addiction. That vile poison wouldn't let her go.

The gang used the vulnerability of Taylor's addiction to trap and traffic her in the evilest of ways. After breaking her body, they broke her spirit by convincing her that her sins were so reprehensible that her parents would never want her back, and no man would ever want to marry her. She believed them when they told her there was no way out. As much as we tried to offer hope, she wouldn't accept it. To Taylor's heroin-soaked mind, there was no going back to Troy, to that brown brick colonial home where she'd had her birthdays and Christmases. She felt unworthy because of the evil she had participated in to feed the demon of her drug habit.

We still pray that, somehow, she will find her way home.

All this is from God, who reconciled us to himself through Christ and gave us the ministry of reconciliation: that God was reconciling the world to himself in Christ, not counting people's sins against them. And he has committed to us the message of reconciliation. We are therefore Christ's ambassadors, as though God were making his appeal through us. We implore you on Christ's behalf: Be reconciled to God.

—*2 Corinthians 5:18–20*

JOCELYN

When we founded Night Angels in 2016, Detroit had at least eight "hot spots" of sex trafficking spread across the city. The dynamics of each hot spot differ in how sex workers operate and how traffickers control their victims. They also differ in the neighborhood environments and level of police presence and law enforcement. The outreach efforts of Night Angels focused on southwest Detroit, where trafficking had existed the longest and was the most highly concentrated. The community had been a predominantly ethnic community where Polish, Irish, Russian, African American, and Mexican immigrants moved to build new lives. Through the years, however, the area became a hub for human traffickers, drug dealers, and gang activity. We felt the Lord leading us there, and He walked with us every step of the way as we ministered there each week.

It's an area most people avoid when they visit the city to attend sporting or cultural events. Everything about it screams warnings of deprivation, desperation, and danger. Tall fences surround properties in an attempt to keep the "bad guys" out. The number of burned-out and uninhabitable houses is alarming. Many properties have been boarded up because either the owners were forced out when they couldn't pay taxes or didn't have insurance or the means to maintain the home or rebuild after a fire. It's not uncommon for our friends who don't have access to indoor plumbing to use the brush-covered walking bridge over the freeway as a quick "potty stop." Emaciated stray dogs and cats wander freely throughout the neighborhoods.

This neighborhood is lined with strip clubs, late-night bars, and one-lane side streets and has plenty of dark corners and hiding places. One of the areas in which we worked has a dilapidated motel on the main artery. The motel appears to be a former Holiday Inn that had been bought and sold several times and had seen its best days many years before. The no-star motel was run by an infamous human trafficker who had turned it into a brothel with more than fifty girls. We knew it was a place where we would see our friends as they came and went. Our hearts would break at the sight of young girls and women sobbing along the side of the building after they had been told to get out and make their quota.

Each week, our team stopped in front of the brothel to talk with the women, offering them our standard lunches and hygiene kits and, most important of all, prayer. The main objective of our work was to insert the love of Jesus Christ between the trafficking victim and the trafficker. Handing out hygiene kits and lunches was often the way into the relationship that allowed us to do that. By showing them care and respect, we earned enough of their trust that they would allow us to speak about Jesus to them.

> **The main objective of our work was to insert the love of Jesus Christ between the trafficking victim and the trafficker.**

One evening, the night manager of the motel got angry with our team because we were blocking one of the driveways that led into the parking lot. Furious, he charged outside and shouted at us to "move along." We didn't feel at all bad about slowing down his illicit business, but we hated to add to the chaos in our friends' lives, so the next week we brought him a large hot pizza and apologized for blocking his driveway. He was impressed. He was always kind to us after that night. Although the evil being perpetrated inside didn't change, the gesture ensured we wouldn't get run off again.

Our first encounter with Jocelyn was just outside the gay adult bookstore only a few hundred feet from the brothel. The bookstore owner was shouting and throwing broken pieces of concrete at her. He wanted her off the sidewalk, as she might be interfering with customers stopping at his lewd business. Talk about irony! We stopped our SUV a safe distance from the bookstore and encouraged Jocelyn to come over to us. She declined.

Ninety-nine percent of the thousands of sex workers we have come to know through the years are *not* the *Pretty Woman* portrayed by Hollywood. Jocelyn was an exception to this rule. What a look this young lady had! She wore stiletto heels, short skirt, and a bustier top that showed off her cleavage. Her petite, shapely body was barely five feet tall and weighed less than 100 pounds. With lots of bling, heavy makeup, and a high ponytail that flowed halfway down her back, she was easy to spot. Even in the coldest months, she wore only a short jacket. Showing off was essential to her work.

Week after week, we saw Jocelyn walking the streets. We would pull up in our SUV and try to engage her, but most of the time she would bluntly say, "In a hurry. Don't have time to talk to you." Sometimes, due to the drugs, she either wouldn't respond or didn't seem to understand that we were trying to reach out to her. We persisted with her. We even tried to appeal to her with compliments.

The women on our team would comment on how beautiful she was, how pretty her jacket was, or how cute her shoes were. Those compliments occasionally got her attention, but she continued to give us the cold shoulder. Still, we refused to give up on her.

After many weeks, Jocelyn's resolve to ignore us broke down, and she came over to our vehicle upon our approach. Exhausted, she decided to trust us after all. She took a sandwich and accepted our offer to pray for her. It was through her prayer requests that we were able to piece together her story that reminded us that truth can sometimes be stranger than fiction.

SEEKING APPROVAL

Jocelyn had been an only child. Raised in a blue-collar suburb of Detroit not far from the Detroit Metropolitan Airport, she attended a strict Catholic school through the eighth grade before switching to public high school. She talked at length about her early religious education and shared her memory of taking her First Holy Communion and being confirmed in the Catholic Church.

When she went to high school, she took full advantage of her newfound sense of freedom from the strictness she had experienced as a young child. She hopped on a rip-roaring ride into the party life, dabbling in illicit drugs and dressing to catch the boys' attention. She laughed as she remembered that, even in middle school, she had made the most of her uniform by rolling the waistband of her skirt and unbuttoning her oxford blouse as soon as she left school each day in an attempt to show off her budding figure. Jocelyn took the opportunity in high school to break out with tight skirts, high heels, and blouses that had the boys in school noticing her every move.

Jocelyn enjoyed school, not for the algebra, geometry, history, or science but for the parties, football games, and social life. She made the dance team her senior year, and her popularity soared. She enjoyed the affirmation she received from the boys in her classes and even from her parents who heaped on compliments about her looks and social status.

Although she was pretty and popular, Jocelyn had extremely poor grades and no serious career or job aspirations. She told us that her parents didn't bother her about her grades. The combination of her complete lack of academic focus and her parents' ambivalence regarding her schooling or future made her fail so many classes that she didn't graduate. In a last-ditch attempt, she started GED classes, but she didn't follow through to complete her certificate.

With no diploma or GED, the people in Jocelyn's life told her she'd never get a job. She decided to prove them wrong by securing employment at one of the popular strip bars located near the airport. These clubs are just far enough off the main routes that people traveling to the airport might never see them or know they're there. With enormous neon lights, large water fountains at their entrances, and billboards featuring specials and pictures of near-naked dancers, thousands of customers and millions of dollars have no trouble finding these palatial establishments.

Jocelyn started as a barmaid delivering drinks, but it didn't take long for the club's managers to determine that her looks and outgoing personality would serve them better on stage. They persuaded her to try pole-dancing first, semi-clothed. When the establishment dismissed local ordinances against nude dancing, the "barely there" clothes came off. Jocelyn not only didn't mind the work, she thrived on it. When her parents questioned how she was earning so much money with so little education, she claimed that she was earning great tips as a waitress. More than the money, though, Jocelyn liked the attention she received as a dancer. She later confessed to our team that her need for attention and affirmation had been her Achilles' heel all along. Shining in the spotlight gave her a high, and she enjoyed it.

SEEKING ACCEPTANCE AND SURVIVAL

Within that euphoria, Jocelyn got introduced to two things that would forever change her life. The first was hard drugs. She had dabbled with drugs as early as age thirteen, but at the club she graduated to more addictive substances, including quaaludes, crack cocaine, and heroin. Although the management at strip clubs might not be directly involved in getting girls high for their exploitation, they create an environment that allows for others to do so—and then the club owners reap the benefit of dependent employees. Lynn, a dancer who was only a few years older than Jocelyn, introduced her to heroin shortly after she started working at the club. Lynn's boyfriend was a drug dealer who gave her all the best things that a life in organized crime could offer: a new BMW, beautiful clothes, and plenty of bright, shiny bling. From eighteen-year-old Jocelyn's vantage point, Lynn had it all. Snorting heroin was a way to fit in and be like her new friend. For several years, Jocelyn was able to keep her drug addiction in check. She could stay high and work at the club while balancing a life that seemed somewhat normal around her parents and friends.

The VIP room was Jocelyn's second, life-altering introduction. She had been dancing at the bar for about a year when Lynn and the management convinced her to work in the VIP room. The work included nude lap dances as well as sex. Jocelyn found it easy, especially when she was high on the drugs that blocked out a sense of fear or guilt; besides, she reasoned that she could work fewer hours each day because she earned so much more money in the VIP room.

Money wasn't enough, though, to fill the void that the drugs and sex work were creating in her life. Nothing seemed to help—or last for long. Every time she bought a nice car, she cracked it up in an accident. Every time she met a man in the bar that she was attracted to, she concluded the relationship was meaningless. By this time, she had moved in with Lynn and had no real relationship with her parents. They continually tried to communicate with her, telling her they missed her and wanted the best for her, but she avoided seeing them.

Several years of sex work in the VIP room and her growing drug addiction took an emotional toll. To cope, Jocelyn went from snorting heroin to using it intravenously. Her looks suffered from the poison she continually put into her body, and since she was no longer their "pretty woman," the management at the club fired her. For a couple of years, she worked in sleazier establishments that offered topless or nude dancing, earning less money and being expected to perform more degrading sex acts. Her drug addiction and the abscesses on her body from using dirty needles caused her to get fired over and over, even from these bottom-feeder strip clubs. She finally resorted to seeking out sex work on the streets to sustain the drug addiction that now controlled her.

Up until that point, Jocelyn hadn't been a victim of human trafficking. Certainly, the people who ran the clubs had manipulated and used her for their gain, but no one controlled her. Seeking work on the streets quickly changed that fact. She was scooped up by the infamous trafficker and his team of kingpins who operated out of the motel where we first met her. For several years, Jocelyn survived by working for the brothel.

SHIFTING PERCEPTIONS

In 2017, six months after beginning our work in Jocelyn's neighborhood, we received a request from the Detroit Police Department (DPD) to meet the captain of the Special Victims Unit (SVU) at the new DPD headquarters. This new facility on the southwest side of Detroit seemed state-of-the-art compared to the dilapidated building on Beaubien Street that we had visited when we launched the ministry just a year earlier. As we met with the captain, it was clear that the location and the building weren't the only things that had changed.

For many years, the police harassed our team during our Monday night outreach work. Officers would see us on the street, and despite their awareness of what we were doing and why we were there, they would shine their car spotlights in our faces and yelp their sirens when they were behind us in traffic. One of the scariest moments our team experienced during our ten years in ministry occurred when officers surrounded our SUV. It was like something out of a television crime show, with lights and guns flashing in our faces. Our team's driver turned on the SUV's interior lights and calmly directed us to put up our hands. The officers said they thought we were buying drugs from the young man with intellectual disabilities to whom we had stopped to offer a sandwich. We didn't see a SWAT helicopter, but in the commotion, we expected to see one flying over any second.

The encouraging meeting we had with the SVU captain felt like a breakthrough with the Detroit police. He talked to us at length about our relationship with the police and what Night Angels was trying to accomplish. It was clear that he cared and was interested in working together toward our mutual goal of helping our friends on the street. For the first time, it seemed that the perception about our friends on the street was shifting. Rather than throwing everyone into the catch-all category of "hookers," the captain and his team recognized that many of these people were victims of human trafficking. They also seemed to understand at least some of the challenges the women and men caught in sex trafficking face. When we mentioned our suspicion of child prostitution, one of the captain's fellow commanders commented, "Things are often worse at home than they are with a trafficker."

During that meeting, we shared our knowledge and concern about the motel, especially about the minors we had seen there. Approximately four months later, law enforcement from multiple branches and departments descended on the motel. Representatives from several social service agencies were on site as well. The bust made headlines in local and national newspapers. Media followed the story as the trafficker, who ran the prostitution ring but had escaped the raid, was finally arrested and prosecuted for sex trafficking.

> It takes a long time for a trafficking victim to trust anyone enough to allow themselves to be helped.

That incident marked a change in the way the DPD dealt with street prostitution. It was the first time we had ever seen the police treat sex-trafficking victims not as *hookers* or *street whores* but as people who need help. Forty-one of the women and girls they'd picked up were released and directed to assistance programs to help them get out of the life and deal with their drug addictions. Despite law enforcement's best efforts to help our friends, most of the victims didn't trust the police or the assistance agencies. It takes a long time for a trafficking victim to trust anyone enough to allow themselves to be helped.

The relationships we had built with the women from the motel had enabled us to earn that trust. Our team continued to work with these women. Over the next several years, we were honored to be able to help thirty-eight of them leave the neighborhood and get their lives back on a path toward the plan and purpose God intended for them.

Jocelyn wasn't at the motel during the raid, but she continued working on the streets, even after the motel-brothel was busted. Occasionally, she took the bus to visit her parents, get a shower, and eat a hot meal, but she always returned to the streets. Her addiction took priority in her life and continued to make her vulnerable. This time it was a male friend, Terry, who took over control of Jocelyn. He took the money she earned from sex work and used it to buy drugs to sustain their mutual habit. When Terry died of heroin overdose a couple of years later, Jocelyn became the property of the drug dealer. This man used Terry's death as an opportunity to increase her addiction and dependency on him. He gave her drugs but demanded swift payment and used violence to ensure she delivered.

Week after week, we saw the progression of the scratches and bruises that revealed the abuse to which she was being subjected. One Monday night, Jocelyn told us she'd had enough. In her words, she "was sick and tired of being sick and tired." It was a phrase we had used several times in our discussions with her over the years. We were happy to hear her use them as she expressed her desire to be freed from the world in which she had been entangled for so long. We took her to detox and then to a long-term drug-treatment program, but within days she relapsed and returned to the neighborhood. She found shelter in what had been one of the best

Coney Islands in Detroit. That place had once served chili dogs that were out of this world, but all that remained was the business's sign and the hull of a building. Squatters and addicts, including Jocelyn, took up residence on the top floor of the empty structure. The shelter offered no running water, electricity, or heat.

It was during this time that we learned Jocelyn had a son who lived with her parents. As is the case with most of our friends, the facts of her story continued to expand over time as we earned her trust by patiently listening to and mentoring her. Terry was the biological father of the child but had never taken on that role. The control of the traffickers and the drugs was too much for Jocelyn to cope with. She couldn't care for herself, let alone raise a child alone. Her parents had stepped into the role Jocelyn had chosen to vacate and adopted the little boy.

On top of all the other chaos going on in Jocelyn's life after her relapse, she became pregnant again (probably from one of her dates, although we don't really know). Jocelyn gave birth in the Wayne County Jail after she was arrested on an old drug paraphernalia charge. She immediately signed over guardianship of her new baby to her parents, and they began caring for this second grandchild.

It took Jocelyn two more rounds through the cycle of detox, rehabilitation, and relapse before she was finally able to break free from the addiction and regain control of her life. Today she lives in a suburb of Detroit and sees her children regularly. She has a steady job in an auto-parts manufacturing plant where she operates a milling machine. Her life is far different from the one she had as a dancer or on the streets. What hasn't changed is her vibrancy. She is lovable and colorful and still sports her bling.

As she works to reconnect with her family and friends in her sobriety, our team continues to pray for her. We want the best for her, including sobriety and healing from the scars she carries as a victim of sex trafficking. We know her best hope is believing that Jesus adores her and choosing to seek Him over and above the approval or acceptance from others.

> She opens her arms to the poor and extends her hands to the needy.
>
> —*Proverbs 31:20*

BELLA

Bella was an exotic beauty. Her flowing black hair, her blue almond-shaped eyes, and her willowy frame reminded us of the imagery of Egypt's Cleopatra. Her inner beauty was equally striking. Her issues hit close to home, and her story reminded us that anyone can become vulnerable to the insidious tactics used by traffickers.

Protected by loving parents, Bella grew up in a Christian home in Rochester, Michigan. Part of that protection was to shield her from the world as much as possible. They home-schooled Bella in elementary grades and sent her to a private Christian high school. Bella grew up loving the Lord and participating in a number of extracurricular and church activities. She played the piano, studied French and German, played soccer, and even sang in the church choir for Easter and Christmas services. Bella's family loved her, her pastor extolled her virtues, and her friends described her on social media as the best kind of Christian friend. Bella seemed to have the kind of life that made everyone around her proud to be acquainted with her.

Bella attended a local Christian college in Southeastern Michigan. Still under the scrutiny and guidance of her parents, there was no wild partying, no staying out late, no getting involved with the wrong crowd. When she met Rod, her parents approved of their new relationship. He seemed like the kind of guy any parent of a young, innocent girl would love to have dating their daughter. Rod was respectful of Bella and her family, and her mother took an immediate liking to him. After a brief courtship, they became engaged and were married less than a year later at Bella's home church.

Rod had attended the same Christian university as Bella. His degree, although not a degree from a seminary, had prepared him to take on ministerial responsibilities for a vocation. Rod's home church thought so highly of him that they offered him a position right out of college to begin his expected lifetime of ministry. Both Rod and Bella were ecstatic to be able to remain in the geographic area, live close to both sets of parents, and start their married life together.

Their idyllic life seemed picture perfect, but the couple immediately began to feel the rumblings of friction in the marriage. Within two years, the issues manifested fully. Bella had been an incredibly submissive child, but as she became a young woman and wife, she desired to step out of the template of her parents' expectations. When she got married, she wanted to wear makeup and clothing that was more fashionable than she'd been allowed to as a child. But in their new church home, where Rod served as a minister, church members viewed Bella's new look as a sign of rebellion.

THE BREAKING POINT

The pressure on Bella that she felt to conform was suffocating. It seemed as if everything about her was up for scrutiny—from her choice of eyeshadow to how long she wore her hair to whether her dresses were long enough. The congregation questioned whether Bella was called to ministerial life and, concurrently, whether Rod was a capable pastor if he couldn't *control* his wife. After all, they reasoned, how could Rod minister to others when things weren't right in his home?

In response, Rod joined the chorus of the critical voices aimed at Bella. He, along with her parents, sided with the church's leaders and its gossipy members. She believed the criticism was undeserved and that her style wasn't promiscuous or provocative. She felt that others had no right to question her motives or choose her wardrobe, but it seemed everyone Bella loved was ganging up on her. The constant badgering and the whispering that went on behind her back wore her down; finally, she suffered a nervous breakdown.

Completely distraught and overwhelmed after another fight with Rod about what the church thought of her, Bella walked out of the house. She left with little money, one credit card, and no extra clothes. Tears streamed down her face as she walked past many stoplights, crosswalks, and storefronts. She didn't know where to go, only that going back home to endure more criticism and undue shame seemed untenable.

Just then, a man driving past pulled over and asked if he could buy her a cup of coffee at a small restaurant that was back at the last traffic light. She agreed. Bella's upbringing had taught her to see the best in people, so when he offered to take her to a shelter for the night, she was thankful for the help.

Bella saw the man as a kind stranger.

In reality, he was a sex trafficker. He saw Bella as a beautiful, sad, and vulnerable woman. He saw her pain and planned to exploit it.

The man quickly began the grooming process. He bought Bella clothes and great meals. Little by little, he introduced her to drugs. First marijuana, which she had never tried, and then other drugs infused into her drinks. The substances took the edge off the emotional pain she felt—and made her even more vulnerable to the sex work he had planned for her.

He saw her pain and planned to exploit it.

Within a matter of days, he upped the stakes and ensured his control by giving her heroin intravenously. Then he put her on the street. Bella's looks and innocence made her an incredible financial prize to the trafficker. Many times, women as attractive as Bella first get trafficked into pornography. This guy must not have had those connections because he immediately put her on the street—the lowest, ugliest, and most dangerous form of sex work. But he knew she couldn't run once she was addicted to heroin. He supplied her with a rig (the syringe, needle, and tourniquet combination), showed her how to inject the drug, and promised to supply all the heroin she needed—for a terrible price.

FAR FROM HOME

The neighborhood he took her to looked like a war zone. Abandoned buildings were boarded up and tagged with gang graffiti. It was nothing like the "safe" Michigan city where she had lived with her husband.

Each Monday evening, we dodged landmines of broken glass and gaping potholes as we ministered to those living on the battle-worn streets, where evil seemed to be winning. We found Bella on one of those streets. She was sitting on the steps outside a tired church building. The neon glow cast by the nearby liquor store highlighted her desperation. When we called her over, she didn't trust us, at first, refusing our offer of the hygiene kit and lunch. Linda, a friend we had met on previous outreach visits, was stationed in front of the liquor store and hollered over, "They're okay. They're the church people." Our reputation had preceded us.

Linda's reassurance and the hunger pangs of having gone without food for three days were all it took to draw her to our SUV's window. We handed her a lunch and hygiene kit, and as she ate the sandwich, she told us she was a Christian, too, a pastor's wife in fact.

Bella relayed the awful story of how she ended up on the street with the trafficker's demand that she prostitute herself. Her sin was so egregious to her, all she could do was sit outside this church building and pray between dates. The fear of being beaten by her trafficker kept her from crying out loud, so she sat silently and prayed. Later we learned from our friends that Bella was regularly being beaten by her trafficker because she wouldn't perform the acts that were required. She often failed to satisfy her dates and, as a result, failed to earn the money her trafficker demanded. That's when the bloodiest of beatings happened.

When we asked Bella that night if we could pray for her, she begged for our intercession. Her body shook from the shame and the toll of the drugs on her body.

The next week, we counted on the light from the neon sign at the liquor store to shine in the direction of the church building so that we might spot Bella again. She was there, and this time ran up to our SUV with no hesitation. She opened up to us a little more. Although she believed the Lord could forgive her, she didn't think her husband and congregation would ever be able to look past her sin. Twyla reminded her that no one is without sin and how no one dared to throw a stone at the woman caught in adultery. Bella thanked us, but she wouldn't be persuaded that night; instead, she hugged us, leaving the wetness of her tears on our cheeks.

The following week, we learned from Linda that Bella had been found dead in a dumpster outside the liquor store. She had overdosed on heroin. The rumor was that she was so unfamiliar with how to shoot up with the needle, she had done it wrong. Twyla broke one of our team's rules and got out of the SUV to hug a scared Linda. The neighborhood was quiet that night. A sense of sadness filled the air as many came to us for prayers for comfort, safety, and freedom from this life on the streets.

Our hearts broke for Bella that night, but we knew she was in God's hands. We knew we were, indeed, in a war zone. Bella was a casualty in the battle with this enemy called sex trafficking. Her story stayed with us. Each time she comes to mind, her life and death remind us of our purpose to minister to the wounded, the forgotten, the unloved, and the brokenhearted by representing Jesus to our friends on the streets.

Bella's story hit close to home. The pastors' wives on our team shared that they, too, had felt the pain and crushing guilt that can come with the pressures of always having to do, be, wear, and say the right thing. Bella felt as if she were suffocating, and her escape led her into danger. Her fear of further rejection by her husband and congregation kept her in danger.

Were her sins too terrible to be forgiven?

Not for the God we serve.

Perhaps Bella knew that and found His comfort as she prayed on the steps of that empty church building. Even in the depths of darkness, she drew as near to God as she felt she could. We pray that she has now found His presence and eternal peace in Jesus's arms.

"If we confess our sins, he is faithful and just and will forgive us our sins and purify us from all unrighteousness. If we claim we have not sinned, we make him out to be a liar and his word is not in us."
—I John 1:9–10

ROSIE

An essential and powerful weapon in the fight against sex trafficking is awareness not only of the reality of this crime but also of its many warning signs. To arm people with this information, we've spoken to countless groups about how traffickers gain control of unsuspecting victims. It was because of one of these events that we met fourteen-year-old Rosie.

Gail sat in the audience, and her skin started to crawl. As she listened to the ways traffickers select, groom, and manipulate young girls, she had the sinking feeling that her boyfriend's daughter, Rosie, had become the target of a human trafficker. She went home, found our contact information online, and called to ask for help. She explained her concerns to Twyla, who, after hearing a little about the situation, agreed Rosie might be at risk. The next day, we visited the family at their home in a middle-class eastern suburb of Detroit.

Gail lived with her boyfriend, Jim, in a well-kept ranch-style home. Jim was working on his ATVs in the garage and immediately came out to greet us when we pulled up to the house. Like

Gail, he had some serious concerns regarding his daughter's safety, and he expressed his gratitude for us meeting with them. Jim invited us into his home, and we sat at the kitchen table with him and Gail along with his parents, who happened to be visiting from out of state. We asked if Rosie's mother would be joining us, but Jim said that although he had invited her, she had chosen not to attend. From Twyla's call with Gail, we knew that Jim and Rosie's mom had been divorced for several years and had joint custody of their daughter.

WARNING SIGNS

Jim called Rosie into the kitchen, and she joined us at the table without complaint or resentment. She did, however, avoid making eye contact with us; instead, she focused on the multiple cats that stalked the room and demanded to be noticed. Because she wasn't looking at us, we could watch her without making her feel any more uncomfortable. We noticed that she seemed a little immature for her age in that she didn't wear any makeup, her short hair was a mess, and her clothes seemed more disheveled than trendy. At five foot, four inches tall and a little overweight, her pale skin was clean, and she looked healthy.

Jim took charge and began detailing the events that, over the previous several months, had troubled him as a parent. The first had been when Rosie had gone camping for a week during the summer with a friend's family. Jim received a call from the friend's parents when Rosie's boyfriend, a twenty-year-old man named Sanjay, showed up at the campground. The fact that Rosie had a boyfriend, much less one that was so much older, was news to Jim. He immediately left to pick up Rosie from the campground.

On their way home, Jim questioned his daughter about her relationship with Sanjay. Rosie told him that she had met Sanjay six years earlier playing the video game *Fortnite* online. Since then, Rosie and Sanjay had chatted through the game, social media, and later through the mobile phone he had purchased for her. Again, Jim was surprised. He had been led to believe that his ex-wife got the phone for Rosie and paid for the ongoing service.

The more Rosie opened up to Jim, the more concerned he became. She told him that Sanjay had recently begun traveling to Michigan from his home in Ohio to see her. Unbeknownst to Jim, Sanjay had sat just a few feet from him at one of her softball games. He had also met her and her friends at the mall several times in recent months. Rosie told her dad that Sanjay liked her to try on clothes that made her feel pretty and had purchased several things for her. When Jim asked to see the clothes, he discovered that most of it was in the closet at Rosie's mom's house and included clothing from trendy stores as well as stiletto heels and even lingerie from Victoria's Secret.

The one question on which he couldn't get a straight answer from Rosie was whether their relationship had gotten physical. Jim wasn't sure he wanted to know the answer. He was terrified about what might be happening in his young daughter's life.

Jim said that when he spoke to his ex-wife about his concerns, she told him he was overreacting. Rosie's mom didn't believe there was a problem; in fact, she liked the fact that Rosie had a boyfriend at fourteen.

Jim was angry. Not with Rosie, but with the twenty-year-old who he believed was, at best, taking advantage of his daughter, and at worse, had much more nefarious plans for her. His anger drove him to the police. He described the relationship between his teenage daughter and this twenty-year-old adult who lived out of state. Jim believed Sanjay had been using the mobile phone to stalk his daughter and that the man's intentions were evil.

The frustration he felt when the police told him the relationship was "nothing to worry about" only compounded his fear-driven anger.

Believing his daughter was in grave peril from someone he believed to be a predator, Jim went full speed ahead on his own to find out who Sanjay was. He was determined to keep his daughter safe, even if he had to do it alone. He started by limiting her access to the family computer and taking away the phone Sanjay had given Rosie. Then Jim turned the tables on Sanjay and used the phone to track *him*. But Jim didn't have to go far. Using the Find My Friends app on Rosie's phone, Jim discovered that Sanjay was sitting in a late model Mercedes Benz parked just outside his home. Jim decided to get a photo of the car and of Sanjay, but when he came out of the house, Sanjay sped away. Jim and Gail pursued Sanjay in their pick-up truck and got the photos that they needed.

Infuriated at Jim's attempt to keep him from Rosie, Sanjay did everything he could to stay connected to her. He mailed clothing and gifts to Rosie at her mom's house. Taking advantage of the access he had to Rosie there, he would make plans to meet up with her at the mall, movies, or after-school events he knew would be unchaperoned.

THE LOVING TRUTH

Rosie sat quietly at the table as Jim shared all of this. His fear, concern, and even anger were evident, but so was his love for her—and it was clear that she felt that, even if she didn't believe him; finally, Jim breathed out a heavy sigh, as if telling the story exhausted him. Gail put her hand on his arm and looked at us. "We just want to know; do you think there's any chance Sanjay is a trafficker? We don't want to be the 'mean' ones, but something just doesn't feel right about this."

The truth is, we agreed with Jim and Gail. So many things seemed wrong about the entire relationship. There is nothing mean about being concerned for the people you love, and we told them and Rosie that. We didn't want to crush the girl's feelings by telling her that her first boyfriend was a liar, but we wanted her to know the facts. We also wanted her to know that she wasn't alone. We had seen young girls in similar (and worse) situations many times.

> There is nothing mean
> about being concerned
> for the people you love.

We explained that what Rosie viewed as romantic or loving expressions were probably Sanjay's way of grooming her for the world of trafficking. He had gone to great expense and trouble to gain access to Rosie—far beyond what would be considered normal or healthy. It is not normal for boyfriends to spend thousands of dollars on their fourteen-year-old girlfriends. It is not normal for a twenty-year-old man to date a fourteen-year-old girl. He told her he cared about her, but he avoided meeting her parents and family. If his intentions were wholesome and morally upright, why would he not want to meet them? The fact that he had attempted to control her by giving her a phone—that gave him the ability to track her whereabouts—was truly suspect.

We made these points as gently as we could, but Rosie dropped her head in embarrassment. Jim and Gail got up and surrounded her in a hug. It was clear to us that evening that Rosie finally understood her father and Gail's concerns. More than that, after our discussion, she realized Sanjay's motives and tactics were nefarious.

Twyla asked Rosie if she could pray with her. Up until that point, Rosie had been stoic, but as they prayed together, her tears dropped onto the kitchen table. Privately, Twyla asked Rosie if Sanjay had forced himself on her sexually. She didn't directly respond to the question, but after their prayer asked her father to take her to see the priest who had administered her First Holy Communion because she needed to talk with him about something.

Rosie made another request of her father that night: She wanted to live with him and Gail full time. Jim choked up. He wanted nothing more and told her as much. Her mother would have to agree, but as they talked, both Rosie and Jim felt that her mother would consent. Rosie's mom, it seemed, was focused on many things, but Rosie wasn't one of them. In the meantime, they agreed to collect the clothing and other gifts from Sanjay and take them to the local charity shop the next day. And Jim destroyed the phone that evening.

Later, we learned that, from the license plate in the photo he had taken of Sanjay's car, Jim found the owner of the vehicle and his address. Armed with that information, he went back to the police who, thankfully, agreed to look into the issue. They contacted the owner of the car who turned out to be Sanjay's father, who, incidentally, was a well-respected professor at a university in Ohio. Sanjay's father pleaded with the police, assuring them he would handle the matter and that the girl would never see Sanjay again.

BACK ON TRACK

We don't believe for a minute that Sanjay was courting Rosie for romantic reasons. And had Jim and Gail not intervened, Rosie's story could have had a different and very evil end.

The truth is, it is especially difficult to get trafficking victims to self-identify when they've been manipulated to believe their traffickers care about them. We will never know if Rosie was raped, sexually abused, or trafficked by Sanjay. We have known girls of Rosie's age to be grossly abused by traffickers in all kinds of nefarious ways. We like to think that all that was averted, but we aren't sure of what might have been the level of sexual activity in which she was engaged—either in her relationship with Sanjay or with others that Sanjay may have made part of his evil scheme. We want to think the worst didn't happen, that she was not used by a single trafficker or a group of traffickers; however, the time when Rosie was unsupervised at her mom's home and Sanjay had access to her is when the unthinkable could've happened.

Rosie's father, Jim, knew something was not right with the relationship Sanjay had with his daughter. The age difference was only part of it. Sanjay had too much money at his disposal. The car may have been his father's, but the cost of the clothing, the trips to Detroit, the shopping sprees with Rosie didn't match the allowance of an unemployed son of a university professor.

Whatever Sanjay may have planned was thwarted before any more damage was done. We share Rosie's story for several reasons. First, because awareness matters. Jim and Gail's willingness to arm themselves with information regarding the potential warning signs and paying attention to what didn't seem right could very well have saved Rosie's life. Second, because it's important to understand that human trafficking can happen to anyone. Rosie was a middle-class Caucasian girl with parents who loved her. Even her mother, whose naivety left Rosie more vulnerable to Sanjay's ploys, cared about her and ultimately did what was best for her by allowing her to live with Jim. Rosie wasn't someone most people would put in the "at-risk" category, but she definitely was. As so many of our friends' stories show, anyone can become a victim. And third, we want to show you that victims' lives can return to normal. With

Sanjay out of her life, Rosie went on to mature into a strong young woman who was able to recognize the difference between healthy and potentially dangerous relationships.

We want to show you that victims' lives can return to normal.

One might argue whether Rosie was a victim—or if she was about to be; regardless, because of a parent's concern, her derailed train was put back on the right track.

"For my Father's will is that everyone who looks to the Son and believes in him shall have eternal life, and I will raise them up at the last day."
—*John 6:40*

TERRI

Drugs and trafficking are evil partners. Sometimes drug use leads to trafficking, as addiction makes people more vulnerable to exploitation. A desperate person's need for shelter, money, or the next hit are often the inroad traffickers take to secure the power necessary to control their victims. And as we've seen too many times to count, traffickers will often administer drugs to those they victimize. They know that getting someone hooked on illicit substances makes them easier to control.

Hard drugs, like heroin and crack, are tools of the trade for traffickers and the downfall of many victims, but that's not necessarily where people's addictions begin. Sometimes, many times, in fact, it's the substances that are viewed as harmless that truly are a gateway into hell on earth. Marijuana is one of those substances. At the time of this writing, twenty-four states have legalized marijuana for recreational use. Debates continue across the United States both for and against outlawing this drug. Those who object to the legalization of marijuana's recreational use cite reasons ranging from its unknown long-term risks for the body and mind to the difficulty of regulating its use to the fact that the body is the temple of the Holy Spirit and should not be corrupted. While we see merit in these arguments, one of the big reasons we are concerned about making marijuana more easily accessible is that thousands of heroin addicts we've met through the years have told us they smoked marijuana long before they ever used heroin.

Such was the case for Terri.

Terri was from Caseville, Michigan, a small town in the thumb of the mitten that outlines the state of Michigan. The perfect place for a cottage on Lake Huron, this quaint village has as many summer-only residents as full-time citizens. Terri, however, grew up in Caseville. Her parents separated when she was young, and although her dad paid the required child support, he wasn't involved in her life in any meaningful way after the contentious divorce. Her mother often picked up extra shifts at the auto-parts factory where she worked to make ends meet. With no grandparents or other family in the area, Terri was on her own much of the time.

She had a part-time job, went to high school, and spent the rest of her time with her boyfriend, Roy. Terri's mom probably believed her daughter was doing just fine. She was cute and charismatic, and her average grades and polite demeanor seemed to indicate she was good at following the rules. But without the strong guidance of family and with no spiritual foundation of which to speak, there was nothing to guide Terri as she traveled down life's road. Her moral compass had never found its true north.

Terri and Roy began experimenting with marijuana in high school. Although plenty of people smoked weed, it wasn't legal in Michigan at the time, so they got their supply from the local drug dealer who operated out of the high school parking lot. During their four years of high school, Terri and Roy were frequent customers, and their dealer encouraged them to experiment with amphetamines and barbiturates for different effects. Had they stuck to marijuana, their lives might have turned out differently; instead, the crescendo of drug use led them down a difficult and dangerous road.

As soon as Terri and Roy graduated from high school, they got married and moved to a western suburb of Detroit, where Roy found work at one of the Big Three auto manufacturers. Luckily for Roy, he was hired before the company instituted pre-employment drug testing at his plant. The job paid well and made it possible to support Terri and their growing family, which quickly included two children. Having grown up with just enough to get by, the pay and benefits were more than either of them had ever dreamed possible. The money also kept them in supply of an assortment of recreational drugs, including the heroin to which they had graduated and were using regularly.

A CHAIN REACTION OF TRAGEDY

Six years into their marriage, Roy overdosed and died. That terrible event sparked a chain reaction of tragedy, beginning with Terri's parental rights. Although getting high was something Terri and Roy had always done together, Roy's parents blamed her for their son's death. They pursued custody of their grandchildren, declaring Terri an unfit mother. Terri fought to keep her children, but the courts denied her requests and blocked her from having contact with them until they turned eighteen.

Alone and depressed, Terri curtailed her drug use but started drinking heavily. Even though she had argued in court that she was not the cause of her husband's death, deep inside, she believed she was somehow responsible. She supported herself financially by tending bar, but when she wasn't working, and sometimes even when she was, she drank to forget the overwhelming feelings of guilt and sadness.

Her drinking binges often ended when she blacked out, which not only scared her but also led to her losing her bartending job. Realizing that one devil was just as bad as the other, she walked away from alcohol but supplanted it with drug use. (She later told us she quit alcohol "cold turkey," which is quite a feat. It has been our experience that detoxing is harder on an alcoholic than detoxing a heroin user.) She took a job at a small strip club in nearby Garden City, Michigan, but this time, instead of tending bar, she was dancing nude and performing sex work. The citizens of Garden City fought to get the club closed as a nuisance, and eventually won, but for Terri, it was too late. The strip club had introduced her to the world of sex work and effectively built up her tolerance for its evil powers.

When the club closed, she moved to sex work on the streets in a neighborhood where our Night Angels team ministered. Sex work on the streets often happens, quite literally, *on the streets*. The "Johns" who buy sex in our neighborhood won't spend the money for a hotel room but usually have sex in a car out in public, partially camouflaged by bushes, a field, a building, or even a dumpster. Terri often hosted her dates behind a liquor store near a dumpster, where police wouldn't easily spot her.

She still needed to earn enough to support her drug use. No longer was it recreational; it was a full-blown addiction. She was snorting heroin and using it intravenously, as well as smoking ten rocks of crack a day. Her desperate need for drugs made her an easy target for the trafficker who ran the bordello out of the old motel. The same man who had enslaved Jocelyn (described in a previous chapter) took advantage of Terri.

STAYING ON THE STREETS

When we met Terri, she was in her forties, but from a distance, with her platinum-blonde hair, thin frame, and skimpy clothes, she could pass for twenty. Up close, though, the ravages of long-term drug use on her face and body were obvious. She tried to smile in a way that hid the fact that she was missing all of her teeth. She was gaunt and flat-chested to the point that she appeared as if she hadn't gone through puberty—which was a selling point to her customers on the street. Aside from that, however, she always appeared clean. Working out of the bordello gave her access to a shower. Something she didn't have in the *bando* where she slept. A *bando* or *abandominium* is a boarded-up, abandoned house, and of course is without running water, electricity, or heat.

The chaos of the streets removes the possibility of permanency when it comes to shelter.

The chaos of the streets removes the possibility of permanency when it comes to shelter. Terri moved from the bando to a tent between two buildings on our ministry route. When we later learned her tent had been stolen, we were reminded of God's perfect timing and loving care when He provided Night Angels with a tent that we were able to give to Terri along with blankets and tarps.

Terri lived in that tent an entire summer before she was sold to a new trafficker who put her up in an apartment building on the main street in our outreach neighborhood. Her new apartment had lights, running water, and heat. She also said that her upper-level apartment had "fewer rats than my neighbors on the first floor." We often thought that Terri must have been a favorite of her trafficker to be given such a comfortable place to crash.

Of course, that arrangement changed, too, and Terri lost her apartment after several months. Her next place was an abandoned car in the vicinity. She even invited a homeless man to hang out with her in the car. He was about her age, and they often used drugs together—a repeat of the lifestyle she missed having with her husband. Incredibly, this man died of a drug overdose while he was in the car with Terri—another repeat of her former life that left her further traumatized. Many of the people who lived on the street, both trafficking victims and the homeless, were incensed at this tragedy and blamed Terri for either buying bad drugs or not doing everything she could to help save the man's life. Some even threatened to kill her over the incident. The Detroit Police investigated the man's death but did not arrest her.

VARIATIONS OF EXPLOITATION

Terri's life was never her own again. She had been bought and sold by traffickers who kept her on the street in exchange for the chemicals her body depended on.

She also fell victim to traffickers with cameras and internet access. One was a pervert who went around the neighborhood making YouTube videos of our friends on the street. He paid the girls ten dollars for an interview during which he would ask them to describe the sex acts they performed. He claimed he was trying to "peel back the onion" of progression into his interviewees', sordid lives, but the reality was just another person exploiting our friends for his own lustful gain. We found it interesting that, at the time he was filming his videos, a deck or hit of heroin cost ten dollars, the same amount he offered for an interview.

When COVID came on the scene, Terri disappeared from the streets. We followed her Facebook page (yes, trafficking victims have Facebook pages) and found out that she had begun doing cam work. This kind of sex work was taking off, and it meant that Terri's controller set her up in a low-end hotel room with a computer, a high-tech microphone, and studio-grade lighting. With these tools and a system developed by organized crime, people could pay to connect to Terri's live camera feed and watch her engage in various acts. It's doubtful that Terri ever saw any of the money, but we postulate that the flow of drugs continued enough to keep her under control.

The last time our team saw Terri was before COVID. She was strolling down the street wearing a white fluffy minidress and seemed happy about how she looked and life in general that night. For all the tragedy in her life, Terri never completely lost her charisma. Each time we saw her, if she was lucid and recognized us, she offered a friendly, toothless smile.

After COVID, we heard a rumor that Terri had been killed by someone who blamed her for the death of the man who had overdosed in the car with her. But we don't really know if that story is true, and although we've heard it repeated a few times by different people, we haven't been able to verify it. Hoping for the best, we watch her Facebook page and pray that she is as happy now as she was the last night we saw her.

We have to wonder whether her life would have turned out differently if she and Roy had never smoked their first joint or experimented with drugs. How might they have ended up if heroin wasn't part of their story? Some might argue that her life was already on a road of dysfunction. Perhaps that's true. Or perhaps, had they chosen a different path, Terri and Roy could have turned things around. Perhaps they would be celebrating their children's graduation from high school and looking forward to the next phase of life.

Sadly, we may never know.

In addition to all this, take up the shield of faith, with which you can extinguish all the flaming arrows of the evil one.

—*Ephesians 6:16*

AISHA

Some women have a knack for getting what they want—and going about it in the nicest way. Unlike the "mean girls" of middle school or high school, these women possess a winning combination of looks, brains, charisma, and interpersonal skills that combine to create a magnetic and persuasive personality. People simply like them.

Hollywood used to call these women "*it* girls," as in, they had *it*—a special undefinable yet undeniable quality that charmed audiences. It doesn't matter if she is the girl next door or the woman in the corner office, this girl (or woman) can talk people into doing just about anything for her—and they'll be happy about doing it. All we hope for in return is the gift of a smile from the ever gracious *it* girl.

Aisha was an *it* girl. We met her on a relatively calm, early summer night. Standing on a street corner in one of the tough neighborhoods we served, she didn't seem to have a care in the world. Part of her calm was the effect of being high on heroin, but as we got to know Aisha, we realized that calmness was part of her personality. She was wearing a long flowing summer dress, and the setting sun shone through the sheer material to reveal that she wore nothing else. As much as that shocked our sensibilities, that, too, we learned was Aisha.

She was only about five feet tall and less than 100 pounds, but her charming personality filled the space around her and shone brightly through her smile and exotic features. Her long dark-brown hair testified to her Egyptian and Chaldean heritage, as did her dark eyes and golden skin. But it was her smile that really drew people in. While many of our friends had significant dental problems because of their drug addiction, physical abuse, poor dental care, and malnutrition, Aisha's smile looked perfect. More than that, her smile was genuine and contagious. When she smiled at you, you couldn't help but smile back.

Over the coming weeks and months, our team developed an incredible relationship with Aisha. We learned that she was from West Bloomfield, Michigan, an upper-class suburb of Detroit. As a child, she had attended church with her family, and she still seemed to have some level of relationship with the Lord, but in recent years, her life had taken a spiraling downturn from which she couldn't seem to recover physically or emotionally.

PRESCRIPTIONS TO EXPLOITATION

As with so many of our friends, drug addiction was her pathway into sex work. After having back surgery a number of years earlier, she was prescribed OxyContin to manage the pain during recovery. At the time, she was married and had two children whom she loved, so of course, she tried to fight the addiction, but the drug took control.

Eventually, the doctor stopped prescribing the pain reliever, so she sought out a drug dealer in West Bloomfield to keep her in supply. When it became too expensive to sustain her increasing addiction to OxyContin, her dealer offered to transition her to heroin. He could see that her relationships with her husband, family, and friends were disintegrating, which made her even more vulnerable to his next offer. He connected her with a local pimp who could *help* her get the money she needed to support her habit. The pimp was small time. This pimp only controlled a few girls, but he operated a human-trafficking ring in Oakland County and, most likely, paid Aisha's drug dealer a finder's fee for the *referral*.

In this pimp's employ, Aisha's sex work took her into customers' homes for bachelor parties, poker parties, and high-end fantasies. But Aisha couldn't maintain the semblance of sobriety she needed to perform in these venues. She was in a tailspin. Aisha was sold to a pimp who trafficked several women in our outreach area who were performing sex work on the streets. The new pimp, Frank, gave Aisha a place and hired Leander, a retired pimp himself, to stay with Aisha and provide protection from other pimps, gangs, and traffickers. She paid Frank $500 a day from what she earned on the street and spent another $200 or more on heroin and occasionally crack. As far as traffickers go, Leander treated Aisha well. We never saw evidence of violence perpetrated against her, and her health seemed relatively stable.

For her part, Aisha knew how to use her charm and personality to manage the chaos of the world of sex trafficking. It didn't matter where she was or who she was with, Aisha was a ray of sunshine. In the dark world in which she lived, that trait above all others made her stand out. As much as we hated that she was on the streets, we were always happy when we saw her.

Unfortunately, her magnetic personality most frequently attracted people who wanted something from her—sex, money, or even a headline. Drawn to Aisha's charm, a freelancer who was writing a newspaper article about "the girls on the street" picked her as the main feature of his story.

When we saw the story in our local paper, we knew that Aisha was being exploited once again. This time it was to further the writer's career. The writer positioned the piece as an investigative story about the life of a drug addict who was using sex work to sustain her drug habit. *And he got it all wrong.*

It was clear to us that the story was written by someone who might, in fact, hire a sex worker. He completely missed the deplorable facts of sex trafficking. Alongside blurred nude photos of Aisha that her pimp had used for advertising in a local underground newspaper, he wrote about Aisha's relatable personality and sweet nature. He failed, however, to notice or care that for everyone who exploited Aisha—from the dealer to the pimps who sold her, bought her, controlled her, and paid her for sex—drugs were a weapon to use against her for *their* gain.

His myopic view was purely to make a case that victims of drug addiction have the inability to work in a traditional job setting, and they turn to illicit ways to make money to fuel their habits. While that can be true in part and in some cases, that limited viewpoint neglects to acknowledge the glaring reality that human trafficking is a multi-billion-dollar industry that uses people and destroys lives. Our friends, like Aisha, are merely tools for the trafficker's financial gain.

'BETTER OFF WITHOUT ME'

Each week we would see Aisha, and each week she brought our team joy with her special personality. She had a genuine sense of compassion and caring and would go so far as to ask for an extra lunch and hygiene kit for a customer she might have with her when our team's SUV pulled up. The only time Aisha refused our interaction was if she was too high to speak with a clear head.

Her addiction was the chain that kept her imprisoned—on the streets and away from her family. Tied to that chain was the weight of shame that comes from the sin and evil that victims of sex trafficking know. It is a burden from which many can't imagine being free. Some believe they are too far beyond forgiveness. Others think there is no possibility of regaining any sense of normalcy with family members. Aisha, like so many of our friends, had been on the merry-go-round of addiction, detox, drug rehabilitation, sobriety, and relapse so many times that she couldn't see a way back to her family. Whenever we tried to get Aisha to open up about her family, she had kind but limited words to share. The one consistent, heart-breaking belief she expressed was, "They are better off without me."

HUNTED AND HEALING

Two years after our first meeting, Aisha disappeared. We asked our friends if they had seen her. We went to the house where she and Leander lived but got no response when we knocked on the door.

A few days later, Aisha was found lying in the middle of her street fifty yards from her house. She had been hit in the head with an axe and left for dead.

When a vicious incident like this happens in the neighborhood, the stories about what happened, who did it, and why start flying. The rumor was that the assailant was a man who had recently solicited and later discovered he had contracted HIV. Our friends said he had hunted her down and attempted to kill her. That was the story on the street, anyway, which means part or all of it may—or may not—be true.

What we do know to be true is that when the local news media picked up the story, the police asked them to withhold the fact that she survived. They were trying to protect Aisha from two things: the would-be-killer and other customers who might also have contracted HIV.

Aisha required multiple surgeries, a long hospital stay, and years of rehabilitation for her traumatic brain injury. Years later, she still has no memory of the violence that was committed against her or her life on the streets. She cannot corroborate our street sources who said the attacker was a customer who had contracted HIV.

The good news out of the terrible tragedy is that Aisha returned not only from the brink of death but from the depths of darkness. She is conversant, healing, and hopefully will be able to piece her life back together with some sense of normalcy.

The world would benefit greatly from this tiny it girl empowered by the Light.

We pray that, out of the evil that befell her, Aisha will step through the open door to regain sobriety, return to her family, and develop a relationship with the Lord. The world would benefit greatly from this tiny it girl empowered by the Light.

"The light shines in the darkness, and the darkness has not overcome it."
—John 1:5

MARCUS

Marcus is a trafficker we met during our ministry whose story needs to be told as a warning and reminder, particularly to those within the Christian community, that spiritual battles often begin early in life. One reason the Lord gave us the community of the Church—both the global body and local gatherings—was so that we might encourage and help others on the road to heaven. The way Christians interact with people—be they others in our church communities, our friends and family members, even the non-believers we encounter—can support them in their battle against evil. In Marcus's case, the interactions he had with believers early in his life seemed to have done the opposite. Worse yet, it was his parents' faith that had a powerfully negative effect. That statement may seem shocking or offensive to some. You might even be tempted to tear this story out of the book and burn the pages, thinking that we're placing blame on "good Christian people" for Marcus's crimes. Rest assured, we are under no illusions that Marcus alone made the choice to succumb to evil and commit terrible sins. We hope you'll bear with us as we share the warnings within Marcus's story and consider how life for him and his victims might have been different.

The evil in Marcus's life found its beginning in a Christian community that never would have suspected the spiritual battle waging in its midst.

Train Up a Child

Marcus grew up in the faith, meaning he grew up going to church; in fact, his parents co-pastored a storefront church on the near west side of Detroit. When his father wasn't at the storefront church, he worked at an automobile factory to support both his family and the ministry to which they had dedicated their lives.

Leading a vibrant congregation of about seventy-five people, his dad preached about the Holy Ghost, while his mom led the church choir and ladies' ministry. For their part, Marcus and his four brothers sat on the front row every service in starched white shirts, ties, dark dress pants, and freshly shined shoes. There was no baseball or basketball for Marcus, no late-night television, few friends outside the church, just "church, church, and more church."

Marcus's parents held the reins tight on their children. Both were strict disciplinarians. The siblings learned to rat out each other according to the honor code their parents had invoked among them—and to deflect blame or negative attention from themselves. Marcus's dad addressed infractions and aberrant deeds in the family's basement using belt whippings as *behavior modification*.

Marcus understood the risks of stepping out of line, so he worked hard to stay out of trouble as a child. Hoping to please his family, he participated in the sacraments of the faith, including baptism, communion, and confirmation. His progression through the steps in the faith may have made him appear to be a dedicated follower of Jesus Christ, but an evil spiritual war festered inside him. He resented his parents for controlling his every move and for the pain inflicted to ensure obedience to them, it seemed, even more than to God.

One way Marcus gained positive attention was through his musical abilities. By the time he was sixteen, Marcus excelled at playing the piano and organ as well as singing. Noticing his interest and ability, his mother groomed him to lead the choir. The congregants followed his direction easily, but Marcus struggled with the communication skills necessary to feel at ease in the role. Sitting in church for hours each week had given him a solid religious education, but the restrictions his parents placed on socializing left him unprepared for everyday interactions. The awkwardness of being a teenager only made his lack of social skills more obvious, both in school and in church. He knew how to direct the choir (and had certainly learned what it looked like to command others from his parents), but simple conversations were a mystery. Talking to girls for social reasons was out of the question.

EVIL TAKES ROOT

By the time he turned eighteen, the spiritual unrest within Marcus had turned into a raging war. The combination of hormones, the stress of keeping up a façade of faith, the desire to be noticed and to be taken seriously as a young man, and the conflicting emotions of respect, fear, and hatred he felt toward his parents created the perfect and terrible conditions for evil to win the battle.

One summer while away at church camp in serene Northern Michigan, Marcus and a few boys decided to play a prank on some of the girls. During an evening recreation time that was only loosely chaperoned by adults, the boys locked several girls in an outdoor bathhouse. Although it was intended as a joke, and the boys were just having fun, the girls were terrified. Marcus came to the girls' rescue and unlocked the door. He let the girls out but kept one of them back. When all the other girls had run off, Marcus attacked the girl. He threw her to the ground and sexually assaulted her.

The furor and consequences caused by his actions were swift and severe. His father, mother, family, and church congregation were appalled. Church and family had been his whole world, so when the church excommunicated him and his father ordered him to leave the family home, Marcus was devastated. Evidently, no one pressed charges, because although he found himself homeless, unemployed, untrained for work, and shunned by every single person in his life, he ended up on the streets rather than in jail.

MARCUS THE TRAFFICKER

We knew Marcus as a trafficker long before we heard his backstory, and what we knew about him made us sick.

"He's over there." Twenty-year-old Tabitha looked in the direction of her trafficker and then back to us. She took the sandwich we offered and then said, "You gotta help me get off the streets."

He was Marcus.

We had been talking with a young man affectionately called the "Hat Man" when Tabitha approached us. (We didn't know his real name, but he wore a colorful, perfectly balanced stack of hats each time we saw him. It was clear he struggled with mental health issues, but he was a big part of the culture of the neighborhood, and we loved him.) It wasn't the first time we had seen Tabitha; in fact, for several weeks, she had come to the SUV window. She was always hungry, always interested in prayer, and always talking about us helping her get away from the neighborhood. Despite our efforts in trying to help her work out a plan to leave, she couldn't bring herself to decide on an exit strategy.

Tabitha made sure we knew where Marcus was because he had a pattern of watching our SUV while we were ministering to

Tabitha with a lunch, a hygiene kit, and a time of prayer. When we pulled away from the curb, he would walk over to Tabitha and take her sandwich. Incensed, our team circled around and waited until he was further away and then went back and gave her another lunch to make sure she got something to eat.

In addition to Tabitha, we believed Marcus was trafficking at least three other girls, Lucy, J-Lo, and Susan.

Lucy was so loving to our team that we all looked forward to seeing her on our outreaches. One of our team members who had experience working with people with autism said she suspected Lucy was on the autism spectrum. She stammered and stuttered severely. She also walked with a limp and had what appeared to be congenital facial distortions. Her unusual looks made her special to us. Lucy panhandled and did sex work for money that she then turned over to Marcus.

J-Lo had been severely burned years earlier when the candles she had been using for heat near her bed started a house fire. She had passed out after using heroin and did not wake up until Detroit firefighters carried her out of the burning house. The fire left her with scars that covered her face and body. Like Lucy, J-Lo was easy to love. She had a kind demeanor, and our team quickly developed a relationship with her. Through our conversations with her, we learned that she received Social Security disability benefits of $700 a month due to the injuries from the fire. Every month, she signed that check over to her trafficker, Marcus.

Lucy and J-Lo were both in their early twenties. Susan was just sixteen when Marcus found her on the streets. (We share her story in a later chapter.)

All four of these young women told similar stories about Marcus. He had laid claim to an abandoned home in the neigh-borhood and kept Tabitha, Lucy, J-Lo, and Susan there when they weren't on the streets. He had placed locks on the outside of the interior doors, which allowed him to keep the four girls sequestered and controlled. Each night, he would lock up the girls and supply their drugs and see to their most basic needs. When they crossed him by not bringing in enough money or simply irritating him, Marcus administered punishment that was far more violent than anything to which his father had ever subjected him.

It's difficult for us to understand the kind of power he held over these girls. All of them told us that he was the very definition of evil, and yet they couldn't bring themselves to make a break from him.

> All of them told us that he was the very definition of evil, and yet they couldn't bring themselves to make a break from him.

One Monday night on outreach, we had pulled our SUV over to talk and pray with Tabitha, when Marcus pushed his way past her to get to the window. We had never met him, but immediately recognized him. Our driver asked him to come around to the other side of the car to talk with him. (It was our policy to have men pray with men and women pray with women when at all possible.) Surprisingly, he did so without complaint. Even more surprising to us was how he opened up when the driver asked how he could pray for Marcus. The man we knew to be a ruthless, controlling, abusive trafficker welcomed the prayer. We were also shocked to learn he had just interviewed to be a worship leader and choir director at a small church on the west side of Detroit. Our team had seen and heard many things during our street ministry over the years, but this night with Marcus and his story coupled with his prayer request left us scratching our heads.

We saw and prayed with Marcus once more before he and Tabitha both disappeared. We continued to see J-Lo and Lucy, who told us that they didn't know what had become of Marcus and Tabitha.

Without Marcus in their lives, both Lucy and J-Lo looked for others to watch out for them. We continued to see Lucy, and she became more of a wanderer. She drifted through the neighborhood and increased her panhandling on a busy street near our outreach area. J-Lo had a much higher level of heroin addiction than Lucy and needed to sustain her addiction. She quickly found a drug dealer who was quite willing to take her SSI check. Her heroin usage was low compared to many—she was using only about $250 per month on heroin. The drug dealer she connected with was glad to take her $700 SSI check as barter for the many drugs that she required. Neither of them ever accepted our help to get off the streets.

Our team continued to reflect on Marcus's story for years, and most of the time our discussions left us with unanswered questions:

What had happened to him to trigger his assault on that girl at camp?

How did his spiritual battle take him from the front pew of the church to an abandoned house where he would lock girls up, beat them, abuse them, and dominate them with narcotic drugs for his financial gain?

Did he return to the Christian church, serve a congregation, and put on the mask of a follower of Jesus Christ?

If so, to whose church did he go? Where is it located? How could a pastor endorse hiring him?

Did Marcus ever have a true change of heart?

Questions, questions, and more questions and no answers other than a sense of peace from the Lord that affirmed our ministry. The Lord just kept telling us to plant the seeds of salvation, faith, love, and hope. So we continued to pray for and feed our friends, give them hygiene supplies, and offer them the hope of Jesus Christ, every Monday, month after month, for many more years.

Commit to the Lord whatever you do, and he will establish your plans.

—*Proverbs 16:3*

PAULA

Little nine-year-old Paula's fair complexion made her look as if she hadn't seen a ray of sunshine in a very long time. She had straight brown hair cut short at her jaw line and parted in the middle. She was thin and liked to wear dresses, especially if they had bows. Those dresses weren't purchased at Nordstrom or Saks but pulled from the racks of secondhand stores and charity clothing closets. The socks she wore with her dresses were usually tattered and stained from infrequent washing.

She was smaller than most children her age, and she lagged behind her classmates. Most of her teachers liked Paula and said she was intelligent; however, she was a year older than the other kids in her grade and always struggled to keep up academically at whatever school she was attending. She was introverted, didn't communicate well with her peers or her teachers, and never participated in class.

One might say that she blended into the background in almost every situation. Few people recognized any sort of trait that made her stand out from the crowd of other children.

By the time she was nine, Paula had been in thirty-one foster homes. Paula's parents had died in a car crash when she was small. She had been left with no other family and had been forced into the foster care system in Wayne County, Michigan. She barely had a recollection of her mother or father. The pain of her grief became an emotional black hole in her life that remained with her as she migrated from one foster home to the next.

There were good foster parents and bad foster parents along the way, but the constant upheaval that came with being a product of the foster care system hindered her academic, social, and emotional development. Although most foster parents are exceptional, there are some who merely want to profit from the system. Paula's stays with good foster parents were so brief that they had not been able to affect her development positively or substantially. She had never experienced the positive reinforcement and affirmation which a family could provide to a young child. Although she did have a roof over her head and some semblance of a decent diet, Paula needed so much more.

Her life was a life without Christ. She didn't know His joy, His strength, and she certainly did not know anything about the love of Christ. And sadly, she didn't know that life could be better. Without the opportunity to develop friendships with children her age, she had no comparison for what seemed *normal* to her.

FAILED BY THE SYSTEM

Paula's problems exploded when she was nine years old, when her foster father began sexually abusing her regularly. At first, she took his overtures as kindness, something she had experienced very little of in her short life. His seemingly innocent pats on her head, kisses on the cheek, and back massages evolved into grievous forms of molestation and abuse.

Her first instinct was to tell her foster mother. When she contemplated doing that, she became fearful of how her foster mother might react. How would her foster mother respond to her telling on her foster father? Would it really make a difference? Could it possibly cause her foster mother to abuse her physically or emotionally? Would her foster mother paint Paula as a liar? Would telling cause her foster father to become even more sexually abusive?

Paula had the moral compass to know that what her foster father was doing to her was wrong. She felt pain and anger when he came to her bed late at night. Her instinct told her to *run, run, run*. She didn't have social or familial resources to turn to, and going to someone in the foster system wasn't an option. None of that mattered to Paula. The only thing she wanted to do was get away from her foster father so he couldn't hurt her anymore. The physical and mental pain of what he was doing to her had become overwhelming. So, courageously, she ran—as fast and as far as she could go.

What were your biggest concerns when you were nine years old? Maybe it was your grades or learning how to play an instrument or doing well in a team sport or what kind of birthday party you wanted to have or fighting with your siblings. Paula's main objective was getting away from the man who was hurting her. All she wanted was to be safe.

Paula had taken a bus once with her foster family, from the Greyhound bus station in downtown Detroit to Cleveland. She knew where the station was, and she thought she could get there by walking and taking a city bus. She thought if she could get on a bus and get away from her foster father, she would be safe. After hour upon hour of walking and the hard work of making bus connections at such a young age, she got to the Greyhound bus station.

The bus station was grimy and more than a little bit scary. (Not much has changed.) It had one place to get a sandwich and a pop, but the bathrooms were dirty and smelled of urine. And the employees of the bus companies aren't too friendly—not even to little nine-year-old girls. The smell of diesel fuel exhaust permeated the confined waiting area, and the people were distracted from one another and even their objectives of getting to their destinations. They focused on reading newspapers and listening to music.

Paula had arrived at the station ready to find a better life. She bravely walked up to the counter and asked the man selling tickets where her seven dollars would take her. His belly-laugh response told her that seven dollars wouldn't take her anywhere. He didn't even bother to ask where her parents were. Paula sat down in the waiting room and contemplated her next move. Silent tears ran down her cheeks as her emotions overwhelmed her. She had no mother, father, or family member to call. No close friend or mother of a friend to provide advice. And unlike most preteens today, she didn't have a mobile phone or way to search for help or answers. All she had was sheer desperation overflowing her emotions with a bleak outlook as to how the next chapter of her life would begin to take shape. Questions raced through her young mind: Where would she go? What would she do? How could she stay away from her foster father?

She spent the next couple of hours mostly staring at the clock on the wall and watching changing shadows as the sun went down. In the hustle and bustle that surrounded her, she heard lots of noise but no answers to her questions.

Out of nowhere, Sam appeared. He struck up a friendly conversation with Paula, asking her where she was from, where she was going, where her parents and family members were. Sam had offered her a cup of hot chocolate and a bag of potato chips out of a vending machine, which she gratefully accepted. She was starving, and the snack hit the spot. Sam seemed like such a nice man.

He wasn't. Sam was a trafficker.

It didn't take much to notice the vulnerability of a tiny, tattered, sad nine-year-old girl. He began the grooming process right there in the bus station by gaining her trust and meeting her needs. No cops were around, and none of the bus station's employees showed any interest in the child. To Sam, the bus station was a hunting ground, and little Paula was fair game.

Sam didn't look like Hollywood's version of traffickers. He didn't look like the bad guys on television. He wasn't flashy with a wide-brimmed hat, fur coat, and gold front tooth. He certainly didn't look dangerous to Paula. He looked more like the manager at the local grocery store where Paula had shopped with her foster mother. An average Caucasian, middle-aged man who was five-foot-five inches, a little chubby, and balding. He wore thick glasses and came across like Mr. Rogers. In other words, he seemed and looked *nice,* not like someone Paula needed to fear.

Sam asked if he could take her for dinner at a nearby Coney Island that had enticed her when she walked by it on her way to the bus station. Her stomach growled at the mention of food, and she agreed to go with him. With that, he completed the second major step of his grooming process: getting Paula away from the location where he had met her. They left in his car. No one in the bus station thought Paula was in any danger whatsoever. Nobody yelled to the bus station management or called the police. No one cared.

Paula herself didn't realize the danger she was walking into when she left the bus station with Sam.

After her hot dog dinner, Paula agreed to go home with him until she could find a better place to live. She was so grateful for his kindness. When Paula got to Sam's home in the city, she noticed it was in a different kind of neighborhood than what she was used to seeing. There were only three or four houses on a full block. The homes which previously existed there had been torn down to reduce blight, so there were not any close neighbors. When Paula entered the house, she was excited to see the two other girls that Sam had told her about, Candy and Clarice.

THIS HOUSE IS NOT A HOME

Candy was fifteen years old and an inch taller than Sam. Her almond-shaped green eyes and sharp features made her look much older than her years. She was pale and thin, and even with stringy blonde hair, she was pretty.

Clarice had brown skin and long dark-brown braids with pink streaks woven into them. She was twelve, half a foot shorter than Candy and barely ninety-five pounds. She had big brown eyes and a lovely smile.

Candy appeared to be running the household. She had been there the longest, and when she gave orders in her Southern drawl, Clarice easily complied. The short skirts, tight tops, and high heels Candy wore weren't things Paula was used to seeing girls wear, but then again, Candy was older. She also seemed distant. Paula didn't understand why, but Candy acted as if she were angry with her when they first met. Clarice, on the other hand, welcomed Paula and viewed her as a little sister. She was happy to show Paula the ropes in this new world and help her learn to live by the rules that Sam would lay down for her. (Paula later came to understand that Candy's attitude toward her was based in fear. The older girl knew that Paula might take her place as Sam's favorite girl. At fifteen, Candy knew she was getting too old to be working with Sam, and she was afraid of what her future might hold. As bad as things were, Candy already had enough experience to know they could get worse.)

In her first few days at the house, Paula watched Sam, Candy, and Clarice interact, and it became clear that this house was not a home. Candy and Clarice had become entwined in an evil and perverted ring of child pornography that Sam produced and distributed. And Paula was to join them.

Each girl had her own sleeping quarters with locks on the outside of the doors so that they couldn't leave their room without Sam's knowledge and permission. In her first few weeks at the house, Sam made sure Paula came out of her sleeping quarters whenever Candy and Clarice were being filmed or photographed. By having her watch before she ever posed or acted for the camera herself, Sam normalized the sex work he would require of her. He further desensitized her moral compass by taking the still photos of her that seemed benign, not all that different from those that might be taken at a family studio at the shopping mall. Through the grooming process, and as time progressed, Paula's modeling went from traditional portrait work to more explicit photos, and then advanced to live pornographic video performances—with Paula as the lead performer.

You might be wondering, if Paula ran before, why didn't she run again? We don't know for sure, but we have some ideas. Sam was the first person who had shown her even the slightest love, counterfeit as it was. He bought her presents and went beyond providing for her most basic needs; in fact, he gave her a better quality of life than she'd experienced in many of her foster homes. She ate well, her clothes were nicer and kept clean, and she bathed regularly. Under his overwatch, she wasn't out in the elements, which can be quite harsh during Michigan winters.

Most of the time, Sam treated Paula well enough. When he became violent, it was usually because he felt Paula wasn't progressing as fast as he thought she should be. He wanted her to appear to be eager in her participation in the pornography being produced. At those times, he would lash out at Paula, whipping her with a leather belt on the backs of her legs until she performed.

He always said he didn't want to do it. She tolerated the abuse as another factor of the general hopelessness of her situation. She even began to identify in a positive way with Sam, a sort of Stockholm Syndrome effect.

Paula developed a strange but, nevertheless, close relationship with Candy and Clarice. The three bonded in a way Paula had not experienced before. Paula didn't go to school, but she didn't mind. School had never been a safe or positive place for her. She didn't miss being bullied by the kids who made fun of her tattered and dirty clothes or her hair that never looked as pretty as the other little girls' braids and curls. Paula certainly didn't miss the dismissive and mean-spirited tone she received from teachers who didn't understand why she couldn't keep up with her academics while being shuffled through the foster care system.

For the next nine years, Paula worked in the world of child pornography production. We cannot begin to fathom the suffering which she must have endured to keep her mental and emotional world glued together. She saw many photographers, cameramen, and other child actors come and go. Sometimes Sam would allow men, who were either part of the pornography distribution ring or who had paid a lot of money, to watch Paula and the other child actors being filmed. Other men came to the house to pick up the materials or to distribute, trade, and sell this most perverted kind of pornography.

Help, however, never showed up.

Sam expanded his business into other parts of the Detroit suburbs, always in isolated residential houses, to keep anyone from detecting the evil occurring within the homes that got bigger and nicer through the years. Sam trapped, groomed, and exploited dozens of children in the process of operating his evil business, and he never got busted, at least not while Paula was with him.

After enduring nine years of sexual, mental, and physical abuse, Paula had become too old to work for Sam. He told her not to worry, he "knew a guy." What he meant was that he knew someone who could further exploit Paula. Traffickers love that trafficking victims don't get used up quickly. They can be used repeatedly in different but equally despicable ways for their trafficker's financial gain.

Sam sold Paula to a successful pimp named Bert, who oversaw a web of high-end prostitution operations all over the United States. At eighteen, Paula became a call girl, working at venues in Las Vegas, Los Angeles, Chicago, and Miami. In the five years that followed, she earned hundreds of thousands of dollars for Bert and his organized crime operation but saw precious little of those proceeds herself. She was kept in upscale hotels, drove nice cars, and had the best clothes and accessories. Wealthy men who used online and private prostitution services hired her for dates to accompany them to parties, events, and of course, to bed.

HAPPILY EVER AFTER?

It was people within Bert's operation that introduced heroin to control Paula when she became too smart and independent. You don't need handcuffs, rope, and chains to control a trafficking victim when you have the heroin needle. Heroin addiction is a strong motivator and helped her depend on and even develop a counterfeit love for her captor rather than looking to break free from him.

You don't need handcuffs, rope, and chains to control a trafficking victim when you have the heroin needle.

Paula was working in Miami at a South Beach boutique hotel for one of Bert's underbosses when she met Matt. The building contractor from Detroit was visiting Miami and wanted to have a good time. A buddy had given him the number for Bert's call-girl service. He called, answered a few questions about his preferences, including the girl's age, hair color, body type, and breast size, and ended up on a "date" with Paula.

When Paula and Matt met, something happened that neither of them expected. They fell in love! As odd as it may seem, that was the beginning of a special relationship that changed her life. Matt helped Paula break free from Bert and his organization and helped her get clean from her heroin addiction. They moved to Detroit, got married, raised four children, and built what appeared to be a normal life.

When their children were in college, Matt was killed in a tragic accident at work. Paula received a large financial settlement because of the accident, but money couldn't relieve the pain of the loss. The trauma reopened that black hole of grief that had consumed her as a child.

Life's problems and emotional challenges can trigger someone to return to their drug addiction even after years of sobriety, which is what happened in Paula's life. After Matt's death, she relapsed to heroin addiction, and with it, fell back into sex work. Her brain associated the two behaviors, so after the money from the settlement was gone, she needed to find a way to earn the drugs her body craved.

It wasn't as if she could call up Bert and ask for a job. Not only had she cut ties with him, but she was also fifty years old—not eighteen. Grey streaked through her thinning, straight brown hair, and her body wasn't in the same shape that it had been all those years ago. More than the normal aging, heavy drug use had wreaked havoc on her body. She weighed less than ninety-five pounds, needed dental work, and her face was marked with sores, an effect of the heroin that looks like acne. Unsteady on her feet, she couldn't walk well in stilettos. Since she couldn't get work as a high-end call girl, she walked the streets of Detroit, where sex workers congregate and where men looking for sex know they can find it on any given day or night.

When we first saw Paula, we thought she might be a soccer mom whose car had broken down on the wrong side of town. She didn't look like one of our typical friends. She wore baggy blue jeans and a conservative blue blouse. Our team pulled over in our Night Angels SUV to offer help and discovered she wasn't having car trouble but *life* trouble. Paula was waiting on that dark street for a "John" to pick her up. We offered her a free lunch and a hygiene kit, instead. Like that little girl in the bus station, hungry and afraid, she welcomed help from strangers.

The truth is, despite all the tragedy in her life, Paula remained kind. She was eager to talk and open to friendship. In so many ways, she didn't seem to fit into the landscape of sex work, but her physical attributes and the visible needle marks from heroin use told her story. We also noticed a medical port near her collarbone. She explained that it was where the doctors were feeding her chemotherapy for the treatment of breast cancer, yet another stress point in her already fractured life.

Each time we saw Paula over the next several weeks, we got to know a little more about her by asking how we could pray for her. Her children were always at the top of her list. We prayed for them and for her, and over time, she came to trust us enough to accept our offers to help her get into detox and drug rehab.

Like so many of our friends, she experienced another relapse before reaching long-term recovery, but as of this writing, she is five years sober—and five years free from breast cancer. Today, Paula owns her own business and has truly become a shining example of overcoming the most difficult circumstances.

That courageous little girl who ran for safety is no longer running, but she is bravely seeking professional help to recover from the long-term psychological problems associated with her past. At the same time, she is helping other trafficking victims find their way to freedom.

Praise be to the God and Father of our Lord Jesus Christ, the Father of compassion and the God of all comfort, who comforts us in all our troubles, so that we can comfort those in any trouble with the comfort we ourselves receive from God.
—*2 Corinthians 1:3–5*

CARISSA

Carissa had been a precocious little girl. The fact that she was small for her age didn't bother her, nor did her need to wear glasses. She preferred reading and science over running and sports, and she thought the glasses made her look studious. She loved to collect bugs, enjoy the beauty of flowers, and listen to beautiful music. This was one little girl who felt comfortable in her own skin.

Some of her confidence came from being exceptionally smart. Her parents were proud of her development as a young child. Once she was old enough to go to school, she advanced much faster than her peers and didn't even mind when they called her "the brain." She took their acknowledgment of her intelligence as a compliment.

Her self-confidence was also bolstered by her parents' love and affection. From Carissa's point of view, life was perfect. Carissa's mom took time to put her beautiful black hair in pigtails before sending her off to school wearing a pretty, long dress she had sewn especially for Carissa in all of her favorite colors. Her father liked jazz and played the music almost continually in their home. Some of her best memories were listening to music while watching her mom prepare dinner before her father got home from work.

When she was in the eighth grade, Carissa's mother and father began to argue. The sparring started at a low level and didn't seem too troubling at first. Over time, though, the tenor between her parents changed, and the tension in her home escalated. Harsh exchanges replaced the beautiful music and brought Carissa to tears, which she tried to hide from her parents. Within a year, the terse words had turned into raging arguments over what seemed like mundane issues. Not knowing how to function in the environment her parents created, she often escaped to her bedroom to find some peace.

Carissa was still a good student, but she didn't enjoy school the way she once had. With all her concerns about what was going on at home, she had trouble concentrating on her work. Each day, she dreaded leaving school because it meant returning home where everything had changed. Aside from the anxiety caused by her parents' constant fighting, she felt a sense of loss in her relationship with them. It had become clear that she was no longer their priority. Her mom didn't have time to make clothes or fix her hair; she had her own struggles as she prepared to go to work herself. Her father spent more and more time away from the house, and when he was home, the shouting matches made it hard to focus. Over time, Carissa's grades declined. Her previously all-A report card became peppered with B's and an occasional C. Carissa's teachers were concerned and tried to talk with her, but no amount of teacher support could fix her parents' marriage.

STRESS FRACTURES

Things took a dramatic turn when a vile fight between Carissa's parents ended with her father packing up his clothes and leaving the house. Carissa was devastated. She was old enough to understand what it meant when her father stormed out. Her worst fears came true when, after a trial separation, a divorce decree permanently divided her family.

The divorce changed Carissa's whole world. Her parents sold the house and divided the marital assets, including their time with their daughter. Her dad had visitation rights, but Carissa lived with her mom in a two-bedroom apartment in a suburb on the rural outskirts of Detroit where the rent was cheaper than the neighborhood where she'd grown up. The move meant Carissa had to go to a new high school. Making new friends wasn't easy, since Carissa was an introvert who had always felt more comfortable with a good book than a good friend. The stress of the situation put her and her mother at odds. They argued constantly. Carissa was generally a good kid and didn't have a boyfriend, so their fights were never about anything major. They just seemed to butt heads about even the most trivial things, like Carissa's choice of makeup, clothing selections, and volume of music that she was playing in her room at night.

About ten months after the divorce was finalized, her mother began dating. Carissa wasn't happy about it, and she wasn't afraid to show it by ignoring the men her mother brought home or allowed to stay over after their dates. Carissa's mother thought her behavior was disrespectful and really didn't appreciate it when her daughter called her out for having men spend the night. It was during this tense time in Carissa's life that her father moved to Atlanta, Georgia, effectively severing ties with his ex-wife and leaving Carissa feeling completely abandoned in the process.

The level of vitriol at home exploded the day that Carissa walked in on her mother and boyfriend having sex on the living room couch. Embarrassed and angry, the boyfriend ran out of the apartment yelling that he never wanted to see Carissa's mother again. Her mother lost her temper and ordered Carissa to leave home and not return.

Carissa began couch surfing, going from one friend's house to another, under the pretense of "spending the night." She was lucky to get three nights' lodging at one home before being asked to move on. This was tough on Carissa, but at sixteen her ability to think about what was in her best interest was difficult. She refused to call her father for help since he had abandoned her. The way she and her mother had separated left her with no possibility of returning. So she depended on short-term help from a few friends, even though she knew her nomadic life wasn't sustainable. Carissa felt a knot tightening in her stomach. How would she survive?

One of her friends, Stephanie, let her stay for a few days. That's where she met Xander. He was a friend of Stephanie's who came to the house a few times to hang out with the girls. He was good looking and, at twenty years old, seemed much more mature than Carissa. He came over one evening while Stephanie's parents were away. They were having a great time, and things got even more *fun* when Xander said he wanted to liven up the party. He offered them pills and marijuana. Both girls turned down the pills without hesitation but agreed to smoke marijuana with him. It was Carissa's first-time to get high. Xander stayed with the girls all evening and left the home in the early hours.

That evening, Carissa felt the pull of attraction. She was delighted, too, when Xander showed what seemed to be genuine interest in her. He asked her about her life, her background, and her relationship with her parents. He didn't talk much about himself, but he was a great listener. When she told him that her mom had thrown her out and she'd been couch-surfing ever since, he said he knew some girls who would be willing to take on another roommate.

What she didn't know then was that Xander was a trafficker and was operating a prostitution ring from a house he owned in an area just west of Detroit. The girls he told her about were other trafficking victims that he pimped out using social media.

Oblivious to the danger she was in, Carissa went with Xander to the house to meet the girls, most of whom were around her age or a little older. Music flowed through the house. When she and Xander arrived, the girls were eating dinner together in the main room. In the past few months, she had often gone hungry, so the idea of being around food sounded wonderful. The idea of having her own room again also sounded great. So great, in fact, that she ignored the internal warning bell that went off when she saw the lock on the outside of the door of the room she was given.

So many things about her new living arrangement seemed perfect. For one, Xander told one of the girls to take Carissa shopping and get her anything she needed. Carissa was delighted. It had been a long time since she'd had any new clothes or shoes, and her makeup had run out months ago. The girl also took Carissa to get her hair braided and styled and have her nails done—truly a luxury. The pampering only enhanced her feelings for Xander. She didn't realize how much she missed feeling cared for.

Xander took her out a few days later by himself and bought her even more beautiful designer label clothing. He also bought her an expensive piece of luggage. She already felt like a princess, but then Xander asked Carissa if there was anything that she wanted or had ever dreamed of having. He told her he wanted to make all her dreams come true. Although she had never taken a violin lesson, she told him what she wanted most was a white Fender violin that she'd seen a musician play at a rock concert. She wanted to learn to play that instrument. Xander knew of a music store in another Detroit suburb, took Carissa there, and bought the violin.

That precious gift sealed the *relationship* in Carissa's mind. Not only was she physically attracted to Xander, but his extravagance blew her away. That night when they were alone in one of the bedrooms of the house, Xander took her virginity. Carissa felt as though she was finally a woman, complete with a significant relationship that was sure to fulfill her dream of having a husband and a family.

SHATTERED DREAMS

Within just a few weeks of giving away her most intimate gift, Xander asked her to "be with" one of his friends. Carissa's shocked mind was unable to process the request or his justification for asking her to have sex with anyone else. Before she could gather her thoughts and voice her refusal, Xander revealed a side of himself that she had not seen before. He told her she belonged to him and would do *anything* he asked her to do—if she didn't, he promised she wouldn't like the consequences.

Xander left her trembling and alone. That's when, finally, the other girls explained the reality of her new life. Xander was their provider. When he gave her orders, she had no choice but to obey. He would tell her whom to be with, when, and where. Most important of all, she had to please the men and do what they wanted so that they would give Xander a good review of her performance on their date. It was imperative that she make these men happy.

Carissa was shocked, shaken, and crushed. Only a few days earlier, she had believed Xander was her knight in shining armor. Now she understood she was a pawn in his evil operation. The girls described in great detail the violence Xander was capable of, and she saw proof taking shape on her arms in the bruises he left when he had threatened her. As the trauma set in, so did fear.

Determined to figure a way out of the situation, Carissa collected coins she found around the house and hid them. Sometimes her dates would leave her a few dollars, which she would stash away as well. When she had enough, she would sneak out and walk to a convenience store about a block from the house and get a pop or a slushy. On her way to and from the store, she passed an auto body shop where she struck up a conversation with a thirty-something-year-old mechanic named Ray. Carissa shared bits and pieces of her story with Ray but tried not to reveal too much. She knew Xander didn't want her to talk to strangers outside of the house, and her roommates had warned her not to bring attention to the house, its occupants, or what went on inside.

CHOICES

Ray had been to one of our Night Angels human trafficking awareness sessions. After only a few short conversations, he began to wonder if Carissa might be a trafficking victim. Ray called our twenty-four-hour hotline and told us about what he had heard from Carissa and the conclusion to which he had arrived. After that call, he also talked to Carissa about our organization. She agreed to meet us at the auto-body shop. If she wanted to go, we were prepared to take her to a safe place. Ray and our team worked out the logistics and went to meet her. She arrived at our meeting place with a few clothes in her new designer luggage and her white Fender violin in its case. Her beautiful brown hair was in braids with expensive extensions. Her nails were freshly manicured with neon polish. Her eyebrows had been arched and tattooed. Her fake eyelashes were extending over her natural eyes. After a short but intense discussion, she let us know that she was eager to get away from this life.

When we offered to take her to a long-term Christian-based restorative care center in southeastern Michigan, she agreed instantly. She quickly began making friends in the care center, attending classes and going to church services. During her recovery, the only time we were able to visit with her and encourage her was during the church services. When we chatted with her, she told us she was enjoying working at the thrift store. All in all, she seemed to settle in quickly.

After several weeks in the program, however, Carissa contacted Xander and asked him to pick her up. Our team was astonished, perplexed, and disheartened when we learned she had returned to her trafficker and life under his control. We knew it wasn't drug addiction that drew her back. So what was it? Was she under some illusion that Xander could genuinely care for her? Had the stress and upheaval in her life caused her to develop a bond with him? Did she give Xander total control over her because he was the one who had taken her virginity? Did she feel a sense of loyalty to the other trafficking victims or think that she could help them by returning? We may never know.

Our job is to plant seeds.
We pray that another one of
God's vessels will come along
and water those seeds.

Our team has witnessed so many unexplainable events and actions that simply don't make sense to us. We must leave them all in God's hands. Our team knows that God led us to Carissa, and we know that we did what the Holy Spirit intended for us to do by trying to help her. Our job is to plant seeds. We pray that another one of God's vessels will come along and water those seeds. Our prayer is that Carissa returns to the plan and purpose that God has for her life—and that He protects her in the meantime.

"You are the light of the world.... let your light shine before others, that they may see your good deeds and glorify your Father in heaven."

—*Matthew 5:14a, 16b*

SUSAN

In an earlier chapter, we mentioned a comment made by an SVU sergeant that struck a painful note in our souls: "Things are often worse at home than they are with a trafficker." Those words resonate in the lives of so many of the victims we've met. And yet, they are still difficult for us to understand.

Everyone on our team had seen the brutality that traffickers exert on their victims. The rapes, the beatings, and the ravages of addiction our friends experienced had become all too familiar. We also understood that traffickers look for and exploit the vulnerabilities of their victims. But to think that our friends' homelives could be so bad that they would choose the streets and their traffickers over their families was a jolting truth that was hard to reconcile with our own realities—even for those on our team who had come from bad parents and ugly home situations filled with all kinds of violence, including sexual abuse. We struggled to comprehend the kind of experiences and suffering that makes trafficking seem like a "better" option for anyone. That reasoning, though adopted by many victims, requires choosing between two variations of debilitating pain.

For Susan, the street seemed like the better option. She was one of the first underaged girls we met on the street. We were new to our anti-human-trafficking mission, and it was several months before we learned she was only sixteen years old. Although the streets had aged her, she had not yet become hardened by their chaos and darkness. She looked reasonably healthy; if she had abscesses caused by dirty needles, they were not visible. She also came across as very bright intellectually.

Susan had light brown hair, piercing blue eyes, and pale skin that turned varying shades of pink in the summer. Although she was thin, she still looked feminine. Her smile was infectious, and her personality was charismatic in every sense of the word. We saw Susan week after week and quickly began to bond with her as she shared her story with us.

Barely more than a year earlier, Susan had been living with her parents and a brother in a beautiful suburban home in Warren, Michigan. Her mother had become addicted to prescription medication and died when Susan was only fifteen years old. Around the time of Susan's mother's death, her brother raped her and began sexually abusing her routinely.

Tragically, Susan believed her brother's actions were her fault—that somehow, she had caused the rape and deserved the abuse that she was receiving from her brother. Despite a good relationship with her father, Susan kept the experience of her sexual abuse from him. She internalized that heavy burden for almost a year and then had a mental breakdown.

DIFFERENT LEVELS OF HELL

That's when she ran. Like so many runaways, Susan didn't have a plan for safety. She didn't have a girlfriend or family member who would take her in. Homeless, she quickly fell into the culture of drugs and human trafficking that existed in Detroit—only about five miles from her suburban home.

A trafficker in the neighborhood, "Marcus, the choir director" (whose story we shared in an earlier chapter), immediately recognized Susan as prey. He locked her up in an abandoned home in the city and immediately began the process of grooming her for sex work on the street. The room that he gave Susan was locked from the outside, and only he had the key. Her history of rape and sexual abuse by her brother made it even easier for Marcus to get Susan "broken in." He typically used violence and rape to train his victims, but Susan easily complied to his demands after he administered the heroin that temporarily relieved her from feeling some of the horrors she was forced to endure.

Marcus, however, mysteriously disappeared from the streets. A new trafficker quickly swooped in and filled the void left by Marcus. Susan's youth and charm made her a high wage earner for her trafficker and a favorite with her customers. In no time at all, Susan developed a large group of regulars. Many of her customers were older men with wives and families in the suburbs, who were willing to risk the threat of AIDS and STDs to buy sex on the street.

Sex on the street is the lowest-cost form of prostitution. Sex bought in strip club VIP rooms, massage parlors, and through call-girl agencies is much more expensive. "Johns" give all kinds of excuses for why they are buying sex on the street, but generally it is to try and get our friends to perform in ways that their wives and girlfriends won't.

The drugs helped dull Susan's pain, and for a while, she treaded the waters of chaos on the street. She even managed to sneak away from her trafficker to visit with her father occasionally, though she knew she would never again live in her childhood home.

A TURNING POINT

Just as the daylight shifted into dusk one steamy Michigan evening, Susan was walking near the abandoned home where Marcus kept her locked up every night. She saw someone rolling the body of her friend Bella into a carpet and then tossing it into a dumpster. Bella, the pastor's wife whose story we shared in an earlier chapter, had lost her life to an overdose that night.

Susan's body convulsed with pain, knowing the indignity suffered by her friend. But the shock of seeing someone who had once been so young and beautiful die on the street and then be thrown away like garbage stirred up raw emotions within Susan. Any small happiness that she had been able to hold onto was snuffed out like the flame of a birthday candle. Only a thin trail of smoke remained to remind her of who she had once been.

The morning after Bella's death, Susan awoke with the determination to change her life and break free from her trafficker's tentacles. She remembered that the ladies in the Night Angels' SUV always said, "When you are sick and tired of being sick and tired, call our number!" And that day, she did.

Our team worked out a plan, and we met her near a restaurant—in a public place with lots of traffic. We had hoped to take her to a Christian-based rehabilitation facility in southeastern Michigan, but at the time, Susan was using heroin intravenously and smoking crack cocaine. Because she was using heroin, we needed to get her to detox first. There aren't many detox facilities in southeastern Michigan, and availability is limited, based on the ebb and flow of federal grant monies allotted to the facilities. The only one we could get her into that day was in Detroit. It was a facility we had taken many friends to in the past—a place where some warned us sexual abuse wasn't uncommon. We had no other choice, so when we dropped Susan off, we fervently prayed with her for her protection and sobriety.

After five days, Susan was still high when our team picked her up from the detox facility. It was incredible that she hadn't sobered up over the five days. We surmised that she must have been using an excessive amount of crack and heroin. By the grace of God, we were able to gain entrance for her at the long-term drug rehabilitation facility that we regarded so highly. The people there were professional and loving. They treated Susan with dignity. They understood that Susan was still high, but they were now able and willing to work with her without further detox. They also understood the limits of what the federal and state governments were willing to provide to addicts under federal funding.

Susan thrived during drug rehabilitation. After many months of treatment, she began assisting in fundraising and awareness events for the facility. Her charisma and communication skills were great assets, and her youth helped her connect with other young people who were suffering from addiction. Every time she shared her testimony at an event, people would come to her afterwards to thank her for her openness and willingness to share.

Evil Pursues

As she progressed through the rehabilitation program, Susan gained more freedom, even while living at the facility. The *sobriety rules* we encourage our friends to follow are "new playground, new playmates, and new playthings." Susan opted not to follow those rules and reached out to some of her former friends from the street. She genuinely cared for them and wanted to see what was happening in the old neighborhood. One of the people she contacted was a much older man who had been a regular.

Delighted to hear from her, the man started sending her packages with snacks and writing materials inside. He even sent packages to her roommates. He attended church services at the facility on Sundays and Wednesdays so he could get a glimpse of Susan. He was not embarrassed to be seen with her, and he won over many of the women enrolled in the program at the facility with his charm. When Susan had a day pass, he would pick her up and take her to dinner and then take her shopping for any supplies she said she needed, even though she was staying at a facility that provided everything that she could possibly need. He showered her with money and clothing and even offered her drugs on her visits with him, which she refused numerous times.

On one visit, he took her to a motel near the facility for an afternoon of partying. Once again, along with an assortment of gifts, he offered her heroine. This time, she gave in to the temptation. She had been clean for many months, so perhaps she believed she would be strong enough to avoid addiction.

It would be just one time. She could handle it.

But she couldn't. She injected the same dose she had used previously, but her body couldn't tolerate it. She overdosed and died in that motel room that afternoon.

Our team loved Susan. We wanted to honor her by attending the funeral service her father had arranged at a small Roman Catholic church that Susan had attended as a little girl.

Unsurprisingly, her brother was not in attendance at the funeral. Nor were any friends from the street, not even the man who had taken Susan to the motel where she had perished.

There were, however, many people asking why she had died so young, so beautiful, and with so much life ahead of her. The priest had questions. Her father had questions. We, too, had questions. Many of them started with *why?*

In the many months that spanned between meeting Susan and standing at her grave site, our team had seen and learned enough to know that the overdose wasn't the sole cause of her death.

Intermixed with the heroin that had flooded her veins was the pain of the loss of her mother, whom she had loved so much and had watched succumb to addiction herself. Alongside that pain ran the trauma of the sexual abuse her brother had subjected her to. She had run away from home so that her brother could no longer hurt her, but the mental and emotional anguish she suffered forever changed her. Though she escaped her traffickers who had treated her as if she was their property and deserved to be abused, they had substantially added to her pain. Then there were the "Johns," the men who demeaned her, violated her, abused her physically and emotionally, raped her again, again, and again, and then discarded her.

Such trauma and loss leave deep wounds, and Susan's wounds never had the chance to fully heal. We were hoping that with more time, the drug rehabilitation facility could have assisted her in healing from her complex layers of emotional and physical injuries. The layers were far too complicated and difficult to process on her own.

Susan left a legacy to our team, in part because of who she was, and in part because of whom she encouraged us to be more like.

Susan left a legacy to our team, in part because of who she was, and in part because of whom she encouraged us to be more like. We had some understanding, albeit small, of what she had been through, and we loved her in the way that we believe Christ loves us. We wanted to serve her, care for her, mentor her, and watch her grow in a relationship with the Lord. But the devil came to seek her out and destroy her.

Her loss felt nearly unbearable for our team. We will never forget Susan—her smile, her gorgeous blue eyes, charming personality, and the kindness she showed to others.

———————————————

Be alert and of sober mind. Your enemy the devil prowls around like a roaring lion looking for someone to devour.
—*1 Peter 5:8*

PAMELA

One gorgeous day in late fall, brothers Jack and Bill were on their way home to Detroit after a run to Miami. The two long-haul truckers had delivered machinery for the government to an Air Force base south of Miami just north of the Everglades and were enjoying the cooler air and vibrant fall colors on the last leg of their trip up I-75 North. They had pulled over for a break at a truck stop just north of the Michigan-Ohio border when they saw Pamela.

As Bill and Jack were walking back to their truck, they witnessed two girls arguing loudly in the parking lot while two of their friends looked on. Suddenly, three of the four girls jumped into a car and drove away. The girl who had been left behind stood, dumbfounded, in the parking lot as she watched her ride pull onto the freeway. Then she began to sob.

The sight of the young woman in distress scraped at Bill's heart. The men approached the distraught young woman and asked her what had happened. Between hiccups and sniffles, she explained that the argument had been about which route to take and where they were going to stop for the night. She couldn't believe her "friend" had just left her there.

STORIES COLLIDE

Bill and Jack didn't feel right about leaving the girl alone. The brothers were members of the "Truckers Against Trafficking" organization and were well aware of the danger of human trafficking for which I-75 was notorious. Truck stops, which often offered adult bookstores, massages, peep shows, and strip clubs with VIP rooms, were frequent hunting grounds for traffickers.

Bill had only recently learned just how insidious sex trafficking was—and that it could even happen close to home. The men were two days into their ten-day trip when Bill had called home to check in. That's when his wife, Virginia, told him an awful story about his sisters-in-law that still had his head spinning.

She shared that her sisters, Ellen and Verlene, were caught up in some real trouble. Both had moved to Detroit from a small town in Kentucky. Ellen had only lived in the city for a few months when she was swept away in a whirlwind romance with Will, the owner of the bar where she worked. Bill's wife had just learned that Ellen's new husband, Will, was forcing Ellen to meet men for sex at motels and hotels in the Detroit area. He was arranging the dates for her at the bar he owned, collecting the money, and beating her if she refused. At the same time, Ellen had confided to Virginia that she felt certain Will was grooming their baby sister, Verlene, for the same kind of work. But instead of beating her, he offered her money and drugs.

Bill's wife was worried sick about her sisters; so was he, for that matter. The story sounded too awful to be true, but he'd learned from his Teamster buddies that Will had connections to organized crime. His instinct and military training were telling him to rush in and beat Will to a pulp. But wisdom told him that he needed to be smart at how he went about helping both women.

All of that was running through Bill's mind when he and Jack found Pamela blubbering in the truck stop parking lot. The guys talked it over and agreed that if they didn't help the girl, it was doubtful anyone else would. So they offered Pamela a lift into Detroit, the next and final major city on their route, and promised to let her off at what they believed to be a good truck stop near their warehouse so she could find her way home.

Although it was the opposite direction of home, Pamela thought the idea sounded better than being stranded in the middle of nowhere. Plus, the recognizable name of their trucking company gave her some hope that it would be safe enough to accept the ride. With the decision settled, the three of them climbed into the truck.

While Jack drove, Bill shared the whole sordid story about his wife's sisters with Pamela. He had been stewing about what to do for the past 3,000 miles.

The drive to Southwest Detroit took about four hours, and most of that time, Pamela just listened. She had never heard a story so terrible. It was unbelievable, but she could hear the sincerity in Bill's voice. Although she had her own problems at that moment, she hurt for him and his family.

Bill and Jack left Pamela at a truck stop near their warehouse, and they parted ways with a smile.

Pamela went inside, found a table at the restaurant, and tried to figure out what to do—continue her trip to Northwest Michigan as planned or find a way to get back home. Either way, she needed a ride.

FROM BAD TO WORSE

Another trucker saw Pamela in the restaurant and offered her a ride to a better place where she could catch the bus and find a place to rest for the night. Since Pamela had such a good experience with Bill and Jack, she accepted the ride from Tito.

Trusting the man turned out to be a life-altering mistake. Tito raped her, beat her, and took her to an abandoned house in Southwest Detroit that was being used by a local gang as a drug house and center for human trafficking operations. Before he left, the gang paid Tito a finder's fee.

Pamela tried to get away, but the gang members brutalized her—raping and beating her while she struggled. They made fun of her Southern drawl and told her she must have been "white trash" down South.

The gang's leader took her driver's license and credit cards and told her to forget about her old name and her former life. She was his property now. Laughing, he said her name would be *Ivory* because she was so white. Although he threatened to ink her street name on her forehead, the gang ultimately decided to brand her instead. Using a metal hanger that had been shaped into their gang symbol and heated over the flame of a propane heater, they seared the brand on her left arm, just above the elbow. The scar on Pamela's pale skin marked her as the gang's property.

The remaining initiation to the gang was equally painful and demeaning. The leader told her she would work the street and how much she should charge for various types of sex acts. He gave her a daily quota for her earnings. Since she wasn't drug addicted at this time, they didn't put the needle in her, and they insinuated that if she cooperated, she wouldn't have to take a beating; however, she would be required to make herself available for sex with the members of the gang without compensation.

EMERGENCY EXTRACTION

When our team met Pamela, she had been on the street for a few weeks. She was sober, which was surprising since most of our friends were routinely high. The twenty-year-old wore cutoff denim shorts, light-colored tank top, and a short pink sweater jacket. As required, Pamela called herself Ivory, and although her skin was pale, she was incredibly dirty. Her short dark hair was oily and in need of a shampoo. She was hungry and readily accepted the sandwich we offered, but she didn't seem to be suffering from malnutrition. When we gave her the hygiene kit and asked her how we could pray for her, she mentioned an infection on her back. Our team has seen infections and abscesses on almost every part of our friends' bodies because of their use of dirty needles, but an infection on the back was pretty rare. Ivory took off her sweater and pulled up her tank to show our team the wound left when members of the gang had dragged her over gravel to demonstrate their propensity for violence. Pieces of stone had become embedded in her back where the infection festered, itched, and tormented her with pain.

> Her tears and immediate trust took us a little off guard because it often took several encounters before a victim would open up to us like Ivory did.

Ivory broke down, crying as she described her suffering. Her tears and immediate trust took us a little off guard because it often took several encounters before a victim would open up to us like Ivory did. She confided that she'd been raped by a truck driver off I-75, then by members of the gang, and she was now doing sex work to keep from being further brutalized by them. Her menstrual periods had stopped, perhaps because of the trauma, but she was afraid she was pregnant. The ladies of our team took a closer look at Ivory's body and could see what they thought was a baby bump. Although Ivory was a little overweight, they felt that her story could be true.

Tearfully, Ivory told us that she wanted out and wanted out right then.

The normal protocol when one of our friends asked for help getting off the street was to create a detailed exit plan. We would thoughtfully and prayerfully decide where, when, and how to rescue the friend so as to minimize the threat to them and our team from the trafficker. But that night we felt the Holy Spirit was telling us to break our own protocols and scoop Ivory up immediately, which we did. We literally hustled her into our Dodge Durango SUV and raced out of the neighborhood.

Since her drug test was clean, our team was able to secure a bed for her in a women's shelter set up for victims of domestic violence. (At the time, there were no shelters in Detroit operating expressly for the benefit of human trafficking victims; fortunately, that situation has changed.) We delivered Pamela, who had told us her real name, to the shelter. Normally, someone from the team would mentor our friends when they went to a detox or drug rehabilitation center. In Pamela's case, though, because the facility was structured to protect victims of domestic violence from their abusers, we could not stay with her. The Lord gave us peace as we left, however. We knew that the rules existed for the safety of everyone in the home. For that same reason, we were not allowed to contact or visit Pamela at the shelter.

Several months later, the organization called to ask if we could help provide a specific type of baby formula for a client they thought we had brought to the facility. Since Pamela was the only woman that we had ever taken there, we felt that the Lord was letting us know that she was free from danger and had delivered a little baby. It was a gift to know that Pamela had found a safe life, not only for herself but also for her baby.

Trust in the Lord with all your heart and lean not on your own understanding.

—Proverbs 3:5

MANDY

When we describe the physical appearance of our friends on the street, we are absolutely not describing the "Pretty Woman" stereotype from Hollywood. Our friends don't wear stiletto high heels, they don't usually wear short skirts, and they don't reveal a lot of cleavage. The normal feminine curves in these women have been distorted by the ravages of heroin and crack cocaine on their bodies. Their female hormones are out of whack. They aren't having menstrual periods, and their bodies aren't functioning properly due to their drug use and gross malnutrition. They typically have abscesses on their arms and legs where they have shot up their heroin with dirty needles. Those needles are often found on the ground and shared by dozens of individuals over a course of several weeks. When our team goes to the street, a filthy and emaciated woman is what we expect to see.

Before taking team members on outreach missions, we work to prepare them for this reality. The last thing we want is to hurt one of our friends by acting shocked by someone's offensive appearance or vile story. We want them to trust us; therefore, we must make a good first impression with them. We want them to see the love of Christ through our eyes and feel the love we have for them: a love without bias, without judgment, without condemnation.

> We want them to see the love of Christ through our eyes and feel the love we have for them: a love without bias, without judgment, without condemnation.

The night we met Mandy, our team was prepared spiritually, mentally, and physically for the rigors of outreach, and we were eager to see our first friend. That night as we pulled up to her, Mandy was standing outside a gentlemen's club that tries to double as a restaurant in our neighborhood. The club had been closed because it had "fallen on hard financial times." Translated in a different way, the club had been busted for serving underage patrons alcohol and allowing lewd acts of prostitution in their VIP backroom. When a club uses the term VIP Room in their advertisements, rest assured that prostitution is occurring within the establishment. There were several other adult entertainment venues on the same avenue, so competition was strong. Even with the closure of the club, the bright lights and neon sign could be seen for many blocks in every direction. Once our eyes adjusted from the brightness, we saw Mandy standing in front of the building, with absolutely no one around.

Mandy was in her thirties and had a milky complexion and long flowing blonde hair. She was almost six feet tall. As attractive as she appeared from a distance, when we got up close to her, we could see how the heroin was taking away her health and squeezing the life out of her body. We could also see that at one time Mandy had been an incredibly beautiful woman. She had high cheekbones and almond-shaped blue eyes, but she was so thin that she had lost any semblance of a figure. We could envision what she had looked like before she had become a trafficking victim. We had seen this story too many times: God's gift of beauty had been stolen by the trafficker.

EARNING OUR STREET CRED

That first night, we pulled our SUV up to the curb near where Mandy stood and offered her a lunch and a hygiene kit. She didn't respond. She just stared out in a different direction and acted as if we didn't exist. We spotted someone in the shadows across the street who appeared to be her trafficker, so we moved on.

For the next two weeks, Mandy used the same faraway stare to ignore us. Our team was undaunted and unoffended. We were determined to soften her. Even when she didn't respond, we told her we loved her and would be praying for her. Usually after a week or two of being approached by the Night Angels SUV, the people who ignore us got curious and asked around, "Who are these crazy church people?" More often than not, we got positive reviews from our friends. We had good street credibility, and no one sensed that we were dangerous in any way. A vote of confidence from someone else on the street was usually all it took to convince new friends to come around the next week and accept our offers of lunches, hygiene kits, clothing, and prayers.

It took Mandy four weeks, but she eventually responded to our consistent approach. She walked over to our SUV to speak with us and accepted a lunch and a hygiene kit. She even let us pray with her. When Mandy took that first lunch and began talking with our team, she was quick to tell us that she was incredibly hungry and hadn't eaten for several days. She certainly looked gravely malnourished. Mandy also told us she was five or six months pregnant. Usually, the female members of our team were quick to discern when one of our friends is pregnant, but not in Mandy's case. Mandy was so tall and thin that her small baby bump was almost undetectable. Revealing her pregnancy gave us the opportunity to discuss a plan to exit her from the streets and get her the help she and the baby needed so desperately.

Her trafficker wasn't around, which gave us the ability to seriously plan her rescue. This was the first time in the four weeks we had seen her that her trafficker wasn't nearby. Mandy only agreed to *consider* allowing us to help her. She said she *might* talk about it during our next outreach. Needless to say, we were disappointed in her reaction, but we also knew the timing of the rescue had to be just right for her, not just our team, for it to be successful.

On the fifth week, we saw Mandy near the same spot we had seen her the first time. But this time, Mandy looked like a sliver of her former self. It was difficult for our team to keep a stoic face. She appeared to be in much worse physical shape. She was hunched over and barely walking.

Her trafficker, whom she called Tom, had hit her face with a brick. The injury would later be diagnosed as a broken orbital bone around the left eye. Her face and eye were bruised and pooling with blood. Her face and legs were suffering from contusions and abrasions. The violence of the injury was further exaggerated by the fact that you could still see a flicker of how beautiful God had made her. Mandy exuded beauty, pain, and the ugliness of violence all at the same time. She willingly agreed to allow us to help her get off the streets.

The first step was to get her to a local crisis center to check the viability of her pregnancy. Mandy agreed to a date and time, and our team picked her up and gave her a lift to the center. The ultrasound indicated that the pregnancy was viable and that Mandy was in her seventh month of pregnancy, further along than any of us had thought. The crisis pregnancy center gave her clothing and vitamins and offered her classes to support her during her pregnancy. We had reluctantly agreed to take Mandy back to the neighborhood after the appointment. She said she needed a couple of days to work out her exit plan with her boyfriend. We didn't like that requirement, but we agreed in hopes that Mandy would allow us to get her to treatment in the following days. Another new revelation was that what we thought was her trafficker was in fact her boyfriend, Tom. When we left Mandy that evening, she promised to call us when she was ready to go to treatment. She wanted her boyfriend/trafficker to agree with her intent.

During our next outreach, we saw Mandy, and she agreed to a time and place to take her out of the neighborhood and get her to a private Catholic home for pregnant mothers. This home specialized in working with women who were seeking help detoxing and emerging from their addiction to drugs in order to care for their children. Our street team was successful in working through the various governmental systems to get Mandy off the street and transported her to this facility without any major problems—and without the interference of Tom. Apparently, he had made a prior commitment that day and wouldn't be around the neighborhood.

During our long ride to the treatment facility, Mandy told her story. Mandy and Tom had met eight years prior while she was working as a dancer in a strip club, much like the one we found her standing in front of each Monday night. She had been in her early twenties at the time, and it sounded as if the gentlemen's club was already trafficking back then. She didn't go into detail about her time at the club, but we have seen many of our friends end up on the streets as sex workers after starting out as a stripper or exotic dancer at a club. Because we had seen this common pattern, we suspected that Mandy had followed a similar path and thought it was likely that she had also picked up her heroin habit from the club owner or a fellow dancer.

COMPASSIONATE HEART. TWISTED RELATIONSHIP.

Tom was about the same age as Mandy, or a couple of years younger. He was not an imposing looking individual. He was rather short, about five-foot-five, of medium build, and his close-cropped hair made him look younger than his years. Tom was deaf and could not speak. Tom went from coming to the club once a week to multiple times per week and eventually almost every day to see Mandy at work.

Mandy truly had a heart of compassion for Tom. Whenever he came into the club, the two of them would interact. They struck up a friendship and started dating. Through technology and Mandy's learning sign language during their dating period, she became quite effective in being Tom's voice in life.

Tom was a BMW mechanic who was doing quite well financially when he met Mandy. They both held high-paying jobs: Mandy at the club and Tom at the BMW dealership. But Mandy introduced Tom to drugs. After several years of drug use, Tom's personality changed. Tom had become increasingly dependent on Mandy, his disability elevating Mandy into an important role in his life. They began living together, and their drug addiction continued to take greater control of both their lives. During this period, Mandy and Tom had two young children, whom they both cared for while their lives were somewhat intact.

Tom began to have problems at work because of his addiction. He lost his job failing a random drug test. Tom had little success in getting work. Most of the time, he could only get hired as a mechanic by the worst auto repair shops. They paid him off the books and never kept him around for very long.

Mandy's health and looks continued to deteriorate due to her heroin use and was fired by the gentlemen's club. They were both hopelessly unemployed. Tom's outbursts of violence worsened as his drug addiction exploded and their finances plummeted.

To make ends meet, Mandy began working in bordellos that were operating out of sleazy motels on the outskirts of the city. That's when Tom moved into the role of trafficker. The money Mandy made kept a roof over the heads of her husband and tod-dlers and kept food on their table. Tom began placing ads for her in the local underground newspapers for sex work, with her photo and physical attributes. He would wait outside the motel or casino where Mandy was engaging in her sex work to drive her to her next booking. Tom took all the money that she earned and managed every aspect of her life. His control was ironclad. He enforced his control with violence when she did not capitulate to his wishes. In this perverted relationship, while he operated as her trafficker, Mandy felt sorry for him because of his disability and tried to make this insane relationship work—especially because of the children.

Mandy's health and looks continued to deteriorate, and she couldn't sustain her reputation with her clientele—she was looking worse each month. Tom decided to take Mandy to the streets to work. He kept the money, he supplied the drugs, and he drove her to and from the streets. He told her when she had to work, he dictated the prices, and he decided when and *if* she could eat. He became merciless as she became his only source of cash. Tom and Mandy were living in a home that was purchased with money from a trust fund his parents had left him at the time of their death. Tom occasionally engaged in criminal activities such as burglary and larceny to make extra money, but he was content to have Mandy take care of him financially.

The ride to the rehab facility was over an hour long, and Mandy was eager to get the help she needed for herself and the baby. She was looking forward to a safe environment and a soft, clean bed to lay her head until the baby was born. She was most excited about a break from Tom's demands on her physically and financially.

Even though the Catholic home wanted to keep Mandy through the delivery of her baby, she stayed at their facility for only about three weeks. In that three-week period, she had transitioned to methadone from heroin. Somehow Tom had been able to continue to communicate with Mandy and came to the facility to plead with her to come back to him. With his empty promises in hand, he picked her up and drove her back to Detroit. We can't imagine the physical, mental, and emotional abuse she suffered during their ride home.

We didn't see Mandy again after she left the facility with Tom. We paused each outreach and hollered her name into the darkness near "her spot" in the neighborhood. She never appeared. We offered silent prayers for her into the night skies.

Approximately five years later, we were watching the evening news reports and learned that Tom had murdered Mandy in their home, with their three children in attendance. Tom killed her with a hammer blow to the head. The act was violent, much like what we had seen in those non-lethal injuries when we first met her. Between the time that we last saw Mandy and her death, Tom had been arrested four times for domestic violence crimes against Mandy. It is incredible to think that a judge permitted Tom's release on bail after he was charged four times in a four-year period. Tom stayed in the house with Mandy's dead body for four days before calling police and turning himself in. Mandy's Mom, when interviewed by the press, stated that Mandy had been victimized so many times that they had become estranged. She told how she had been dominated by drugs and was caught up in a world of sex trafficking with Tom while she struggled to raise her three children—the youngest was five years old, the exact timing for the child she was carrying when we first met her.

Our team saw Mandy's beautiful high school graduation picture posted in the newspapers. We all knew that she was a beautiful person inside as well. She had tried to reach out to Tom and help him through his disability. We felt that beyond his physical disabilities, though, Tom struggled with the demons of self-loathing, drug addiction, and anger. Tom didn't have the Lord in his heart; he couldn't understand Mandy's compassion.

Tom didn't have the Lord in his heart; he couldn't understand Mandy's compassion.

We will always miss Mandy and her beauty.

For he has rescued us from the dominion of darkness and brought us into the kingdom of the Son he loves, in whom we have redemption, the forgiveness of sins.
—*Colossians 1:13–14*

LISA

Being "old" is not a vaccine against catching the virus of the trafficker. Our team has concluded over the years that human trafficking victimizes people of every gender, ethnicity, age, and socio-economic background. No one is exempt. Vulnerability is the open door that traffickers use to enter their victims' lives. They can and do exploit the weak, defenseless, lonely, broken, young, and old for their own financial gain. Our friend Lisa tested the conclusion that age is not a barrier for the traffickers: they reach out and seize a victim, no matter how young or how old.

> **Vulnerability is the open door that traffickers use to enter their victims' lives.**

Lisa had been on the street approximately five years when we met her early in our ministry, and she looked like she was about seventy years old. She worked in one of the worst parts of the city where trafficking flourished. She had not grown up in the city, nor did she really know much about Detroit. But the city had become her home.

Short and grandmotherly looking, she wore her curly blonde hair close-cropped, and the roots always needed a touchup to cover the stripe of gray. She needed a substantial amount of dental work and always looked as if she needed a shower. Lisa's clothing was not provocative; instead, she usually appeared as if she had just returned from a bad shopping trip to Walmart—disheveled and needing rest and nourishment. Lisa's obviously bad health was caused primarily by her crack addiction and by the fact that she had lived many years in drug houses or on the street. It's why we thought she had to be seventy, when, in fact, she was in her early fifties.

Over the six-year period we worked with Lisa, she always seemed to look forward to seeing our team on the street. She would take our food, the hygiene kits, and whatever articles of clothing we brought with great appreciation. She often rushed our prayers along, or skipped them altogether, saying a "special date" would be picking her up soon to take her to a motel where she would be able to shower and clean up. That special date and shower didn't come along very often; however, one night she found us and gleefully shouted, "I just had a date that gave me a 100-dollar bill!"

A "NORMAL" BEGINNING

The more we got to know and minister to Lisa, the more we found out about her former life and her present situation on the street. She told us that her life was relatively normal into her late twenties. As a girl and a young woman, she worked in low-paying jobs, typical to people her age who are still living at home. She got pregnant, but the child's father was not interested in marriage. They maintained a distant relationship, and she allowed him to have limited visits with their little girl, Anna.

Lisa's father had died when she was a teenager, and her mother permitted her to keep living with her after Anna was born. Lisa's mother supported her and the baby with the pension she had earned as a postal worker. Lisa helped with finances by taking part-time retail jobs, but she never made steps toward a stable job or career. Her mom babysat while Lisa worked, and the three seemed to have a relatively stable home life for many years.

When Anna was about ten years old, Lisa's mom contracted cancer. Lisa gave up her part-time job to become her mother's full-time caregiver. She was able to collect money from a federally funded program that paid caregivers for providing care to terminally ill people. For the next five years, Lisa cared for her dying mother.

Anna had developed an incredibly positive relationship with her grandmother, so the loss greatly affected both Lisa and her daughter. Lisa sank into a deep trough of grief and mourning, causing her a high level of mental and emotional anguish; unfortunately, it isn't clear whether Lisa was mourning the loss of her mother or the fact that her mother's financial stability was now gone. She struggled with finances because her mother's pension was no longer there to support the household. Anna was old enough to go to latchkey during the school year, but Lisa had trouble balancing childcare and work issues. She struggled with holding down the steady job necessary to support her daughter. Money was an ever-present challenge.

Lisa's life literally came crashing down on her when she was involved in a car accident two years after her mother's death. She sustained major back injuries from the accident. Because she was hospitalized for a long period of time, Lisa was forced to put Anna in foster care for those ten months. Beyond the myriad of health problems that she suffered due to this car crash, the worst thing that happened to Lisa was that her doctors prescribed opiate-based painkillers to help her cope with the devastating pain she was experiencing. The addiction to those painkillers led her down an evil path.

Once her physical condition had stabilized after the auto accident, Lisa was able to bring Anna to Mom's house once again. Anna returned to the elementary school she loved, and life seemed to be more stable for their tiny family. Lisa, however, was on a long journey to fully recover from her back injury. She went to outpatient therapy for years. A lawyer was busy negotiating a financial settlement for the serious injuries she incurred. That negotiation and subsequent litigation took over two years to settle, but Lisa ultimately prevailed. She received a substantial settlement, purchased a new car, and was able to pay off her hospital debts. Her financial picture brightened for the first time in a long time.

Lisa was on better financial footing, but the type of work she could engage in was limited by her back injuries. She could not lift more than twenty pounds and could only stand for short periods of time. She worked low-paying retail jobs for over two years and was able to manage a reasonable lifestyle for both her and Anna. She attempted to file for a Social Security disability benefit during this period but was denied. Even so, she could pay her bills.

Despite her relative financial stability, she became lonely and depressed. She later told us that she described this period as "my boring life." She had no relationship with God, and she was slipping into addiction. Since her back pain had improved, the doctors cut off her opiate medications. But she was not pain free. She felt desperate. She'd had few friends in high school, and that circle had not gotten any wider in the years since graduation.

DESTRUCTIVE ADDICTION

One of her coworkers from the florist shop where she had found a job introduced her to smoking crack. She saw the drug as a tool to cope with her pain while still maintaining the ability to keep a reasonable oversight of Anna. But over the next year and a half, Lisa acquired a gambling addiction. In just two years, she became addicted to gambling and crack and completely unable to support herself or Anna financially.

Anna's biological father had been watching Lisa's out-of-control lifestyle and the effect it was having on his daughter, including her stay in foster care. He had kept up his relationship with Anna over the years and decided to try to get custody of his daughter. A few years earlier, the father's relatives had reached out to Anna and developed relationships, and the middle schooler had eagerly embraced their attention. It took him several months, but Anna's father gained full custody.

Lisa's loss of her daughter struck her core. Everyone she loved was gone. Her struggles had only brought more suffering. She began to react in harmful ways. She sold her house that she had inherited from her mother and continued to gamble and use crack. Over the ensuing months, she smoked up and gambled away all of the cash from the sale of the home. Lisa soon found herself homeless. She pleaded with her drug-dealing friends to give her drugs and promised to "do anything" that they asked to pay them for the crack that she craved. Her overall health had begun to deteriorate even more than it had before arriving on the streets. Her teeth had begun to fall out, and she was losing weight; she weighed even less than she had in junior high school. Her hair was thinning, and her speech was beginning to slur when trying to carry on a normal conversation.

She was not young and attractive, but she'd said she'd "do anything," so the drug dealers decided to use her age and her "mama look" to influence and control sex workers from the house. The job that the traffickers give women like Lisa is called "a bottom b*tch."

The bottom b*tch performs sex work on the streets for the trafficker, but she also disciplines the pimps' trafficking victims. Her duties include collecting money from victims that the pimps say is owed to them—a high percentage of the cash paid by the John (the person who engages in commercial sex with the trafficking victim). The bottom b*tch may also threaten a beating from the pimp if the victim doesn't provide enough money back to him. She may provide drugs to the victims when the money is delivered to the pimp.

Lisa's age was an asset in this position in which she took on the role of a controller while also being controlled herself. Lisa was good at her job because she had a kind way about her but could issue the wrath of the trafficker when required to do so.

OUT OF THE FIRE

Several months after our first encounter, she had been demoted from her bottom b*tch rank and thrown out of the drug house. We found her lying face down in the street and almost lifeless. The crack habit had truly overwhelmed her, and we thought she might also be snorting heroin. Our team took her to the emergency room at the hospital, where the doctors noted a laundry list of health issues, including pneumonia. She told us at the hospital that before she had been thrown out, the crack house in which she had been living had been shot up in a drive-by. The residents had taken to huddling in the basement and living on the cold basement floor in case street gunfire erupted on the first floor.

When she had recovered from the pneumonia enough to be discharged from the hospital, Lisa returned to the same crack house and begged to be readmitted. We were never sure of what she had done to get ejected, but she was able to get back in. A few weeks later, a blood feud erupted between the trafficker/drug dealer that Lisa was living with and one of his rivals. One evening, Lisa's house was firebombed and burned to the ground. Many people in the house that night were killed, including the trafficker/drug dealer. Firebombings were a regular occurrence in the neighborhood for the following two years, as feuds literally flared up between traffickers, drug dealers, and sex workers. But Lisa somehow emerged safely that night. That's when she decided to call our hotline and ask for help. She wanted to get away from the neighborhood and move on to a new life.

We determined at the time that Lisa was using only crack cocaine; thus, she did not need to go to detox but could immediately enter long-term restorative care. We had a favorite place in southeastern Michigan where we took her, and she flourished in their care. She found a relationship with Jesus Christ and began a plan the counselors had for dealing with her addiction. She stayed in the program for one year and even earned the freedom of working in the thrift stores operated by the organization to help raise funds. This organization was proud of being a faith-based program and never took any federal money for their support nor charged any of their clients for their care.

Upon graduation, Lisa began an additional two-year program, living in a residential home owned by the organization adjacent to their main women's facility. While there, she worked as a cashier in the community at a local supermarket. A year later, she became a supervisor within the thrift store organization and was handling great responsibility. She was able to maneuver the bus system in southeastern Michigan and moved around freely, even socializing and attending church regularly. For several years, she never missed a Wednesday night or Sunday evening church service. She seemed to be on fire for God, and her faith did not appear to be superficial, but deeply rooted. Our Night Angels team had even considered adding her to our volunteer staff and taking her with us on outreach to encourage victims with her "story of success." Best of all, she had rekindled her relationship with Anna.

BACK INTO THE FIRE

After many years of sobriety, Lisa fell back into her addiction and returned to her role as a bottom b*tch for a major pimp in the northeastern section of suburban Detroit. Our team was devastated. We had accepted and trusted her. We are still dumbfounded about Lisa. We literally saw her rise from the gutter to find Jesus Christ and a purposeful life. She had worked through an addiction recovery program and had created a rather normal life again.

As hurt as we were by Lisa's choice, we can't begin to describe the pain Anna suffered when her mother turned back to drugs and life on the streets.

Can people lose their way without losing their salvation? Can someone's return to sin keep them from God's grace? Our team will not judge. We really do not have the answers, anyway.

What we do know is that the pain Lisa's choices caused to herself, her family, and the friends she made within our team will not soon be forgotten; however, they can always be forgiven. We continue to pray that she will find her way back to healing, to family, and to true hope.

Repent, then, and turn to God, so that your sins may be wiped out, that times of refreshing may come from the Lord, and that he may send the Messiah, who has been appointed for you—even Jesus.

—*Acts 3:19–20*

DAUGHTERS

When our team began a ministry to locate and help human trafficking victims, we knew that we were headed for a direct confron-
tation with the devil on his own playground, with his own playmates, and with his own playthings. We knew that we would feel
like outsiders in the deep, dark, and evil world of trafficking. We
understood that there was no training or preparation for what we
were about to do, and no one to teach us what we needed to know
before we dove headlong into the work. We asked the Holy Spirit
to train us, to show us how to minister, where to minister, and to
whom. One of the most gratifying things that the Holy Spirit did
was to give us the ability to show the love of Christ not only to
our friends who had become victims of the traffickers but also to
the gangs and the drug dealers. We also had to learn to operate in
their environment. The Holy Spirit gave us the ability to pray with
the traffickers and with the men who purchased sex on the streets.
We understood that human trafficking, one individual controlling
and using another human being as a tool for financial gain, was
evil personified. The means by which that control was gained—the

use of drugs and violence—was all a heinous act that only the devil could have contrived.

At first, after seeing hundreds and then thousands of victims during our years ministering, we would always say, "Well, we have seen it all." And believe us, we did see evil upon evil that seemed to have no end. Each night after ministry, we would pray and go back to our families. We would return to our work the next day. We would return to the Christian community in which we all served and worshiped, and we would try to compartmentalize the work on the street and the evil which we had seen. Most of our team seemed to cope with that paradigm week in and week out and over the ten-year period of our ministry. Most of our team members stayed with us for long periods of time and stayed committed for the long haul. They remained passionate about the cause of making a lasting positive impact with our friends.

After seeing and praying with thousands of victims of human trafficking, our team was not callous about the work, nor did they generalize about our friends or try and categorize them, as a social scientist or anthropologist might do. Every friend was an individual and was viewed as special in the eyes of God. We didn't just see hundreds of victims in our work; we saw thousands of them over the years. Each one of them got a piece of our heart and a love that the Lord supplied to us with an unending flow from the Holy Spirit. One paradigm that exists and appalls us to this day is the existence of mothers and daughters as sex workers. Everyone knows that it's just natural for a mother to care for the welfare of her children: A mother cat takes care of her kittens, a doe takes care of her fawn, and human mothers will throw themselves in front of a moving truck to save their baby's life. But a victim of sex trafficking will "bring along" their young girls and train them in the business of sex trafficking. Some will sell them and become their traffickers; some will be sex worker buddies with them. It is among the most disturbing and unnatural dynamics we have ever seen. We were never able to understand these heartbreaking relationships. Here we offer five stories of mothers and daughters—all victims of trafficking—who were mutually entangled in the life of sex work.

THANK GOD FOR GRANDMOTHERS

Lynn was a grandmother to Lilly and Sarah. The three of them were walking down the street in the neighborhood in which we were ministering on a Monday night and spotted the Night Angels logo on the side of our SUV. Lynn said she had heard about the work we were doing and told us how glad she was to see us out ministering. Lynn was not involved in trafficking her thirteen- and eleven-year-old granddaughters but shared that their mother had sold them to a trafficker in Bay City, Michigan.

Lynn's daughter-in-law had become an abuser of drugs over time. When the daughter-in-law had become indebted to her drug dealer for a large sum of money, he offered to sell her children for sex so that she could work off the debt she owed him. The girls quickly went to their grandmother with the details of what they were being subjected to. Lynn immediately went to law enforcement and then social services to get custody of the minor children. After a long period of time, Lynn won custody of her granddaughters.

We could hear the passion in Lynn's voice as she shared her story with us. We could also see how much her granddaughters loved her. The whole time we chatted, each girl had an arm wrapped around the older woman. They watched and listened to her with admiration.

Lynn had moved from the Bay City area to southeastern Michigan to get away from the environment surrounding her daughter-in-law and her family, which we completely understood. This was a solution that we suggested to many of our friends through the years. We prayed with Lynn and the girls that evening and gave them hugs and some soft blankets we had been blessed with in which they could cuddle up. Even as we tried to encourage them, Lynn encouraged *us* that night with her example of courage and a commitment to stand up for her grandchildren's safety.

Lasting Consequences

Kayla and Anna were mother and daughter and were both doing sex work on the street in our neighborhood. We would usually see one or both on Monday nights. Kayla and Anna were small-framed women whose skin was pale even in the middle of summer. What they lacked in physical stature and strength they made up for in the harshness of their mouths. They were both hard to love, but our team loved them through thick and thin. We saw them clean and dirty, high and sober, hot and cold, and through all the extremes of the life experiences of a homeless drug addict, trafficking victim, and sex worker. We knew them for years and worked with them to start a relationship with Jesus Christ and to get away from the power of the traffickers and the magnetism of the heroin needle.

Kayla grew up in the suburbs with a good family. The combination of drugs and a series of bad relationships set her on a path down a dark road. She started using drugs in high school and, by her late twenties, had four children by four different men. Her severe drug addiction, however, kept her from gaining custody of any of them. Kayla's parents had tried repeatedly to get her into detox and long-term drug rehabilitation, but she couldn't stick with it and always ended up back in our neighborhood with her trafficker and drug dealer. Some of Kayla's children thrived, or at least survived, with their fathers. Anna did not. She, too, had succumbed to drugs and had followed her mother onto the streets where Kayla's drug dealer trafficked her. Anna had gotten pregnant several times during the period we worked with her. She had aborted some of the children but had delivered some—which she couldn't keep, as they had been taken away by social services due to her drug addiction.

Kayla and Anna's issues and personalities made them difficult to connect with as individuals, and they were especially abrasive with one another at times. Other times, they seemed like the best of friends. Kayla seemed to lack maternal instincts, ostensibly a casualty of long-term drug use and homelessness, but the pair had a convoluted way of caring for one another—one that included sex work as a normal part life.

We prayed with Kayla for years before she finally agreed to go to detox and drug rehabilitation. As of this writing, Kayla has been sober for more than two years and has been working to reconnect with her children. Anna hasn't made her way to sobriety yet, but we pray that the seeds of Jesus Christ that we planted will one day come to full bloom in both of their lives.

STICKING TOGETHER

Dee and Brianna, both friends from the street, are a mother and daughter who have always stood out to us—primarily because Dee is probably one of the most attractive women we have ever seen on the street and has always kept her good looks despite her heroin addiction and chaotic lifestyle. Somehow she keeps her heroin addiction under a level of control that we have not seen others be able to maintain for a long period of time. She still has a bright smile, good skin color, and always seems clean and well put together in a world where good grooming and makeup are rare. She is petite. The ladies on our team often use clothing size to describe our friends, and they all agreed that Dee is a size three. Her long brown hair and small stature made her look like Debra from the television show *Everybody Loves Raymond*. She also seemed to have a voice and intonation like Debra's.

There is so much missing in our friends' stories because they are unable to peel back the layers of their lives.

Dee's daughter, Brianna, is a bit taller and heavier than Dee and didn't seem to look much like Dee, but both women agreed to the mother-daughter connection. Dee and Brianna were never together on the street, but they always asked for prayer and food for each other, which is how we learned of their familial connection. Our team was never able to piece together the "how and why" of what brought the two of them to the street, but clearly drugs were the common denominator and most likely the vulnerability that the traffickers used to groom and control them. We always felt as if Dee, because of her striking looks, probably tail-spun through the gentlemen's clubs circuit or had once worked in the world of pornography—but that was merely conjecture on our part. We never really got the truth. There is so much missing in our friends' stories because they are unable to peel back the layers of their lives. Revealing the truth is too hard for them to deal with. Dee and Brianna seemed to share a strong bond with only a hint of complaints about each other. But we knew that when life on the street became extremely dangerous and difficult, they would stick together as mother and daughter.

TOO GREAT A LOSS

Sarina, Rita, and Sarah are a family of women whom we found difficult to understand and help. Sarina was the mother, and Rita and Sarah were her two daughters. As far as we know, Rita and Sara were Sarina's only children.

Sarina was a tiny White woman in her mid-fifties who wore a silver ring in her nose. The first time we ministered to her was in the month of November—she didn't have a jacket on and was dressed in a tight, short-sleeved blouse. It isn't unusual for our young friends to go without jackets early in the fall season, but she was a little older, so we were surprised that she didn't own a coat. We made a point to bring her a jacket the next week, and when we stopped to give it to her, she asked if we had seen her daughter Rita.

Sarina described Rita as in her late twenties, pale, and five feet tall, normally having long red hair. "But," Sarina said, "Rita got crossways with her 'man' [trafficker], and he completely shaved all that beautiful red hair off her head." Sarina also said that Rita's boyfriend, Benny, might be with her and that he was walking around with tubes hanging out of his arm since storming out of the hospital against medical advice after being hospitalized for an overdose.

Rita and Benny were easy to spot. When we saw Rita for the first time, we couldn't help but notice that her drug addiction and general poor health had caused her to lose most of her teeth.

We met Sarah, Sarina's youngest daughter, a couple of weeks later. She was the spitting image of Rita, but she had a full head of red hair and was a little shorter. Sarah always seemed jittery when we ministered to her, perhaps due to her heroin addiction. We had noticed that sometimes the power of the Holy Spirit, on which we depended, would cause our friends to become edgy. But Sarah was always respectful and prayed with us when we gave her food and a hygiene kit. Sarah was pregnant and had gotten on methadone to deliver and keep the baby. The belief on the street is that if you deliver a baby in a hospital and are an intravenous drug user, the baby will be taken by the state and put into the foster care system; however, if you are on methadone as a maintenance drug while attempting to get off heroin, you have a chance at keeping your child.

We stopped seeing Sarah on the streets as her pregnancy came to term. Rita told us, as we were praying with her one evening, that Sarah was staying with her father who lived nearby. For a time, we held out hope that Sarah had made it off the street; unfortunately, the baby was born drug addicted, and the foster care system took custody of the child.

The next time we heard anything about Sarah was from a distraught Sarina, who told us her daughter had gone back to her trafficker only to die from a heroin overdose almost immediately after returning to him. Sarina dealt with that tragic loss by telling every detail of the morbid tale to anyone who would listen. Rita, too, was devastated by her sister's death. She, like her mother, used drugs to cope with the deep and painful grief she continues to carry. And their trafficker kept them in supply and continues to profit from their weakness.

DELAYED COMMITMENTS

Dawn and Toney were the last of the mothers and daughters that we met in our time of ministry. We met Dawn first on the street and found her to be incredibly kind and clear headed despite her heroin addiction. Dawn (who, we discovered, was Sarina's niece) was emaciated. You could see her ribs and arms protruding from her clothing in the summertime because of her malnutrition. Her skin was always pale, she was probably in her mid-twenties, her teeth were in horrible shape, and she had a dent in her neck that appeared to have been caused by a bullet wound. About the third time we saw her on outreach, she was bald. Her trafficker had shaved her head. She told us that she had accidentally knocked over a makeshift table where her controller was separating and packaging heroin. He got angry, pinned her down, and shaved her entire head as punishment.

Over the next several months, we watched and rejoiced with her as her hair grew back in a beautiful light blonde color. Dawn became pregnant while we knew her and began taking methadone in hopes of keeping her child. She successfully delivered a healthy child but chose to relinquish custody to the father to keep the baby from being put into the foster care system. Dawn told us she was trying to reconnect with the child and had made a commitment to take parenting classes and go to detox and drug rehabilitation. The detox and drug rehab were still on her to-do list.

One day, Dawn introduced us to Toney, her mother. Toney was a real mess. She was an alcoholic and looked to be in her sixties but was probably much younger. She drove a car, which was unusual for one of our friends. She would regularly use her car to drive around looking for Dawn. She also used her car for business. Toney was a sex worker. She would have her dates get into her car and then drive to a side street in our neighborhood to conduct business. In spite of her chaotic lifestyle, Toney was always friendly and would pull over in her car when she saw us to accept a lunch, a hygiene kit, and a prayer. And she always requested prayer for her children, including Dawn.

———————

Only the Lord can reverse the deep hurt and damage caused by this unnatural upbringing. The mental anguish, physical pain, and psychological damage embedded is in each mother and daughter.

ANNELIESE

Marlena heard about our ministry with Night Angels through Christian circles in the Detroit area. She called our hotline because she was concerned that her granddaughter, Anneliese, was in jeopardy of becoming a trafficking victim. Marlena asked if we would meet Anneliese and speak with her before anything happened to her.

We knew from experience that engaging in interventions with victims without first building a trusting relationship with them had a limited success rate. That's true, in part, because people don't always realize or believe they are being trafficked. Convincing them to consider that possibility can take time. But even those who are aware that they are being trafficked may be hesitant to change their circumstances. Fear, drug addiction, or a twisted perception of security could keep someone from breaking ties with their trafficker. It often took weeks or months of outreach interactions with victims to gain the necessary trust.

We couldn't ignore the concern in Marlena's voice, though, so we prayed about her request and decided to give it a shot. Anneliese lived only a few blocks from our home, so we agreed to meet with the family at their home.

Before that meeting, we talked with Marlena at length on the phone. She told us a lot about her own life, which confirmed our decision to get involved with Anneliese. Marlena's parents were of German heritage and had immigrated to the United States prior to World War II to flee the oppression of Nazi Germany. Her family had settled in a German enclave located in the northeast part of Detroit. Marlena grew up going to the same Baptist church her grandparents had. Later, she married her high school sweetheart, Hendrich, at the altar there. Hendrich retired, having been a machinist at a General Motors plant in Warren, Michigan, for many years.

Marlena was full of faith, and her life centered around church and family. She was the church secretary and proudly played the organ and piano for every service. Marlena and Hendrich had two sons, Jack and Michael, and intentionally shared their faith with their boys. Both boys had gone to Sunday school throughout their childhood. When they grew older, they were baptized after making a confession of faith. Marlena stressed to us that she felt that although her children had been rooted in faith, her granddaughter was not. She believed Anneliese's father, Michael, had drifted away from his faith and upbringing over the years (a fact he confirmed when we met with him and his family). She also commented that Michael's marriage to Anneliese's mother, Janice, had some challenges. With a significant amount of background information, we scheduled a time to meet with the family.

When we arrived at Michael and Janice's suburban home, the gray brick colonial with its well-manicured lawn was welcoming. Michael politely greeted us at the open door and invited us into the living room where Marlena, Hendrich, and Janice had already gathered.

Marlena and Henrich, who were seated on the living room sofa, quickly stood and shook our hands. Both were pleasant and seemed kind. They thanked us for being willing to meet with their family. Marlena, an attractive, thin woman in her early seventies, was neatly dressed in a gray business suit and white blouse that looked as if it had been starched and ironed only moments earlier. Her perfectly styled hair was so securely lacquered with hairspray that it would have taken gale force winds to make her look unkempt. Hendrich, who had lost most of his hair, sported thick glasses, a new polo shirt, and dark dress slacks.

Michael and Janice sat on a comfy loveseat without touching. Michael looked like a younger, more athletic version of his father, with just a little more hair. Also like his father, he worked for a General Motors plant in the Detroit area. Janice was a pretty woman, who appeared to be running on stress, caffeine, and nicotine. She was an administrative assistant at a mortgage company in a suburb of Detroit, where she traded long hours for great pay and benefits. Her prematurely graying hair and the creases that had appeared on her face years too early were further indications of stress. Her tired appearance and lack of engagement that evening seemed to be a commentary on the state of her marriage, in-law issues, and certainly the calamity facing them all.

It was good that Anneliese was tardy arriving home, as it gave us a chance to talk to the family first. Michael informed us that he and Janice had tried to engage their daughter many times in the past two years in discussions about her future after high school. Her grades would be enough to graduate, but not good enough to get into a university. Because of Anneliese's unfavorable grade point average and ACT scores, her high school counselor suggested that she enroll in classes at the local junior college to possibly gain entrance to a university in a few years. Michael said they had also tried to explore vocational training opportunities, such as culinary arts, cosmetology, or paramedical jobs. Anneliese, however, had no interest in any of those conversations. Her lack of zeal about the next chapter of her life seemed to be consistent with the way she had approached life thus far. Michael said that, rather than setting goals, "She just seems to ride the wind and do just enough to get by."

That lackadaisical attitude apparently extended beyond her studies to most aspects of Anneliese's life, including friendships and extracurricular activities. The one exception had been her participation on the varsity volleyball team. Anneliese was quite tall, which served her well in the sport. She seemed to enjoy the competition and being part of the team, but she hadn't made close friends. It wasn't that the others didn't like her, but her limited interests made it difficult for others to connect with her. Her teammates talked about their boyfriends, their excitement about going on to college, or their part-time jobs. She simply had no common ground to share with any of them, so from her parents' view, she never really connected with any friends.

We asked about the state of her faith and her relationship with the Lord, and silence fell over the room. Michael and Janice stared at the floor and refused to look us in the eyes. Their reaction gave us the answer. After a minute or so, Michael explained that Janice was Catholic. He had been brought up Baptist, and they didn't share similar opinions about faith. Their divergent perspectives caused a rift early in their marriage and had become an excuse, albeit a poor one, to not pursue the Lord at all. It was clear from his explanation that he felt guilty about the fact that the only church background Anneliese had received came from the few Sundays she'd gone to church with her grandparents. That certainly didn't provide the bedrock of faith necessary upon which to build a life.

Janice didn't have anything else to add on the matter other than to comment that she didn't see how our question had anything to do with the circumstances they were now facing.

WARNING ALARMS

It was July, two months after Anneliese had graduated from high school. Michael and Janice had again pressed Anneliese about plans for her future. Her response set off warning alarms for everyone in the family. She planned to answer an ad she had seen online to be a "shot girl" at a bar near the Detroit Metropolitan Airport. Michael knew that this particular bar was also a strip club. No one thought Anneliese's idea to be a shot girl was a good one.

At first, the family tried to make an unemotional argument to Anneliese that the location was too far away from her home in Sterling Heights; the commute would be an hour each way. Undeterred, Anneliese reasoned that the $25 per hour pay (which was more than three times minimum wage) would be well worth the drive. She pointed out that it was far more than any of her former classmates were earning at their part-time jobs.

Anneliese arrived more than a half hour after we had arrived. She entered through the back door, stomped through the kitchen, and quickly ran upstairs to her bedroom and slammed the door behind her. Michael waited a few minutes and then went up and asked her to hurry up and come down to talk to us. Although she had been aware of the time for the meeting and the fact that everyone was in the living room waiting for her, she took her time getting ready, even taking a shower. She finally came back down-stairs, only to pause in the kitchen to answer a call on her mobile phone and chat while we continued to wait for her in the living room. Eventually, she made it to the meeting. She plopped into a chair near us, stretched out her long legs, and crossed her arms over her chest in a defiant posture. She offered no comment or apology for her lateness.

Anneliese could have won a beauty contest. Even with her hair still wet from her recent shower and without makeup, she was pretty. Her pale skin looked as if it hadn't seen a ray of sunlight despite the fact that it was the middle of summer. And there was plenty of skin on display. She wore a pair of pale pink booty shorts and a white tank top. Her clothes were clean but contained the odor of marijuana, which was still illegal for recreational use in Michigan at the time.

We initiated the conversation by asking Anneliese a few questions about herself. Her defenses had clearly been on high alert, even before she arrived home. Rather than engage in conversation she said, "Look. I'm over eighteen and can make great money serving shots. What is the big deal?"

Her next statement was like a slap in the face to the family gathered around her in that room. "Anyway, I got the job. They want me to start next week."

While her parents and grandparents shook their heads in disapproval, she went on to say that she planned to move out as soon as she had enough money saved up. That started the conversation down a different path, with Michael and Janice asking why she was so desperate to move out. Interestingly, she didn't have a long list of complaints about her family. She just stated that she wanted her independence as soon as possible.

Turning the conversation back to the bar, we asked Anneliese if she knew the place was a strip club that was renowned in the Detroit area, not only for its stage dancing but also for its VIP rooms where customers and dancers went for private parties and lap dances.

"I'm just pouring shots." She rolled her eyes. "I am not going to be dancing."

We had met several friends on the street who had worked at this bar, so we knew how it operated. This bar was high-class sleaze. The large facility that, in addition to the bar, included a stage on the first floor, multiple VIP rooms, and a large back patio that flourished in the summertime as waitresses and bartenders in various stages of minimal attire served its clientele. It was modern, posh, and appeared upscale.

We explained to Anneliese what our ministry entailed and that we were experienced in helping sex-trafficking victims. We told her that we had worked with friends whose downward spiral had begun under very similar circumstances. We also predicted her most likely path if she chose to move forward with this job:

She would work as a shot girl and get used to the vibe in the bar.

As a shot girl, she would get used to wearing scant clothing which would make her volleyball shorts seem like "over dressing."

She would get used to being touched by customers.

Soon she would be laying down on tables to let customers pour shots over her cleavage and belly in the name of entertainment.

The money she earned would suck her into a whirlpool where evil swirled around her.

After a short time, she would see the larger amounts of money that the strippers made and understand that the work of a stripper wasn't all that different from what had become normal to her as a shot girl.

We told Anneliese that she would meet other girls her age who were dancers and strippers who were also being sex-trafficked in the VIP rooms and in high-end call-girl operations. These girls would be part of the trafficker's organization. The girls would seem to have the world on a string, even though they were the ones on a leash held by their traffickers. They would recruit her into dancing and stripping, then ultimately into a life of prostitution. They would use her desire to be detached from her family and her lack of education as a vulnerability to exploit.

The fact that she was already using marijuana recreationally would give them the open door to introduce her to harder drugs like cocaine, crack, and heroin. Once they got the needle in her arm, their control would overpower her.

While her family listened to our predictions with tears in their eyes, Anneliese glared at us as if we were crazy. Rather than argue, she kept silent and remained unconvinced and unemotional. Her body language made it clear that she hoped we would leave sooner rather than later.

A Predicted Path

Less than three months later, Marlena called us again. Anneliese had ignored every warning and had traveled the path we predicted, from shot girl to stripper then to sex work in the bar's swanky VIP room. She had developed a full-blown heroin addiction in that short time. Marlena told us that her granddaughter was doing the "cement floor detox" in the Macomb County Jail, which is lying on the floor of your cell, vomiting, sweating, and cramping with diarrhea while groaning and suffering the effects of detox without medical assistance. She had been arrested during a prostitution sting at a cheap local motel in Macomb County far from the upscale bar where she had gotten the job as a shot girl.

We learned later that upon her release from jail, Anneliese refused to return to her parents' or grandparents' homes; instead, she stayed at the apartment of a stripper who worked with her at the club. The stripper, just as we had warned, worked for the traffickers to help keep Anneliese controlled.

Anneliese restarted her use of heroin as soon as she moved in; unfortunately, like many people who begin to reuse after detoxing, she started using a higher dose of heroin than she had ever used before. Her underweight body couldn't handle the onslaught, and Anneliese died within a week from a drug overdose.

After a funeral service at her grandmother's Baptist church, Anneliese was buried in a neighborhood cemetery just two miles from her childhood home in Sterling Heights. We lived only a few blocks from this victim. Sex trafficking happens in our community, and we guarantee it's in yours.

> Sex trafficking happens
> in our community, and
> we guarantee it's in yours.

WATCH FOR THESE SIGNS

Although we had predicted the terrible path that Anneliese followed to a tragic, early end, the death of this young woman hit our team especially hard. Her story mirrored a pattern that occurs when people refuse to believe they could ever become victims or neglect to heed the warning signs.

One of the most shocking statistics about the sex trafficking victims we met through Night Angels was that **more than 90 percent of the victims on the streets were from the suburbs.** Go back and notice the details in Anneliese's story.

Or Rosie's story.

Or Taylor's story.

Or Bella's story.

These women didn't live on the "wrong side of the tracks." You might not expect that women from their socioeconomic status would be at risk for ever being targeted by a trafficker. But traffickers don't care as much about what a potential victim has as what he or she *doesn't* have. Where there is a deficit—or perceived deficit—the trafficker sees vulnerability. Vulnerabilities expose areas of weakness in the person's heart (emotional state and sense of self-worth), mind (intellect or critical-thinking abilities), and soul (spiritual foundation, morals, or values). Traffickers know they can exploit their victims' weaknesses, so they watch for them. Sometimes they even help create them.

> Traffickers know they can exploit their victims' weaknesses, so they watch for them. Sometimes they even help create them.

Consider the list below of vulnerabilities that traffickers look for in a potential victim:

- Non-existent or weak spiritual or moral foundation
- Few, if any, close friends
- Sub-level grades in school
- Lack of ambition
- Disregard for future plans
- Disrespect for self and others
- Disconnection from family
- Recreational drug usage

In Anneliese's case, her heart, mind, and soul were all at risk. It didn't matter that she came from a nice home in a nice suburban neighborhood. Does that mean she was a lost cause? That she was doomed from birth to fall into the evil snare of sex trafficking?

Could there have been a different outcome? We can't answer that question specifically for Anneliese, of course; however, we have witnessed people's lives take beautiful turns away from—and *out of*—the dangerous snare of sex trafficking, so we refuse to believe that people are *doomed* to this terrible evil.

So what makes the difference? Very often, it is relationship. At the beginning of this story, we noted that we had tried interventions without the benefit of relationship in the past and had seen limited success. But as we took time to establish relationships with individuals during our Night Angels weekly outreaches, we walked beside more than 600 people as they began new lives of freedom. Many of them are still in our lives today. And some of them, like Paula and April and so many more, are not only our friends but have also become our sisters in Christ.

Awareness is essential.
So is actively caring for others.

We tried to warn Anneliese, but many times it is more effective for someone who is closer to the young person to be the one who raises the red flags. Parents, grandparents, aunts, uncles, coaches, teachers, bosses, friends, even *friendly acquaintances* who care enough to get involved and are equipped to identify the warning signs may be able to head off trouble before someone starts down a dangerous, potentially deadly path.

Awareness is essential.

So is actively caring for others.

"Then the righteous will answer him, 'Lord, when did we see you hungry and feed you, or thirsty and give you something to drink? When did we see you a stranger and invite you in, or needing clothes and clothe you? When did we see you sick or in prison and go to visit you?'

"The King will reply, 'Truly I tell you, whatever you did for one of the least of these brothers and sisters of mine, you did for me.'"

—*Matthew 25:37–40*

NURSES

The first reaction most people have when we mention human trafficking is "surely not in the United States." That was our first thought, too, and it was echoed by almost every person who eventually joined the Night Angels team.

We understood that human trafficking occurred in places outside this nation.

We had heard about Christians going to large cities in Thailand to do outreach as missionaries where brothels thrived on selling underage children for sex.

We could certainly believe it happens in South and Central America. The poverty is so great in those areas that human trafficking flourishes.

We had no trouble believing it was happening in nations that had been part of the Eastern Bloc of the former Soviet Union. Yes, that was understandable. Human trafficking could succeed where such oppression had its roots.

It's true that human trafficking exists in all those places *and* right here in the United States; in fact, it is virtually everywhere.

It exists in Detroit, in the suburbs of southeastern Michigan, and all over the state. It may take different forms in different geographic locations and demographic groups, but human traffickers don't discriminate. What they look for is vulnerability of the individuals, and they pounce on this vulnerability for their financial gain.

Our Night Angels team was soon being invited to speaking engagements at a variety of venues in order to raise awareness and understanding of human trafficking in our community. At each awareness seminar, we would get the same reaction from our audience: "Surely not in the United States!"

The stories we shared—like those in this book—highlighted victims from every ethnicity and socioeconomic background, men and women, boys and girls, with ages ranging from nine to seventy, left people in disbelief. We are sure many of them questioned our view on reality. Most of the people we spoke to in middle-class suburbia were blown away by the fact that the problem wasn't limited to the minority communities in lower-socioeconomic areas of the city. People thought that because our outreach ministry was in Detroit, the victims we met on the street must all be Black or African American. When we presented awareness seminars at churches with predominantly Black members, the pastors and congregants were often surprised to hear that most of our friends from the streets were White women in their twenties who had come from affluent suburban families and had become victimized in the city.

We've said before that traffickers seek out vulnerabilities to exploit. A trafficker will masterfully identify a weakness and then develop and enact a strategy to pull the victim in close. Using coercion, usually in the form of violence or extortion, the trafficker will draw the individual into his control and ultimately into the world of trafficking. The most vulnerable are often at some sort of physical, mental, emotional, relational, or financial disadvantage:

- adults in severe financial hardship
- children aging out of the foster care system
- people using drugs recreationally
- people who are addicted to drugs or alcohol
- victims of rape and incest
- individuals in an unstable homelife
- runaways with no plan for their safety
- those drafted into prostitution by family members or others they trust

Traffickers know how to find and exploit people from all these groups, and we heard proof of that fact each time we prayed with our friends and listened to their personal stories.

Many of the people we met during awareness sessions felt that there must be some group, some demographic, some geographical area where trafficking didn't exist. When we told them that if there was a protected group, we hadn't identified it, people's jaws dropped. You can't move to a particular neighborhood; money won't provide a shield; membership in some group or organization will not protect you completely from traffickers. One of the questions we often heard was, "Isn't there an educational level that we can reach that will guard us from the dangers of these predators?" That's when we would usually tell them the story of our two nurses, Tanya and Linda. Their education, professional standing, and money-making capability didn't protect them from trafficking.

Risking It All

Linda was in her late forties when we first met her on the street. She told us that she worked as a nurse at a large, well-respected healthcare conglomerate in the Detroit area. Her work was focused on oncology and bone-marrow transplant medicine on its central campus.

Like many busy medical professionals, she wasn't wearing a lot of makeup and didn't appear too concerned about her hairstyle. Overall, though, she had pretty good hygiene. Her fair skin was clean. Tall and thin, she certainly looked to be in better health and physical shape than most of our friends. The first night we rolled up beside her in our SUV, she was sporting her nursing scrubs, and she told us that she suffered from COPD, bipolar disorder, and severe depression. She confided after several weeks of getting to know us that she had been married for five-and-a-half years and divorced for ten.

Linda had begun her nursing career in the emergency room of the hospital. The ER was a level-four trauma center in Detroit that saw some of the worst cases in the city: shooting and stabbing victims, casualties from car crashes, and women who had experienced some of the most horrific domestic violence imaginable. She witnessed the effects of the sheer ugliness of the most evil and violent aspects of society and had been the one to bandage up the broken.

Her problems began when she started going out with her coworkers after her shift in the ER ended. They typically went to a bar right across the street from the hospital. It was popular with doctors and nurses who, like Linda, wanted to forget the pain they had seen on the job. Most of these medical professionals kept their drinking within relatively safe boundaries. Linda didn't. She had addictive tendencies that continually increased her tolerance and the amount of alcohol needed to achieve the numbing effect she desired. Not only did she drink more than most of her peers, but she also used crack cocaine to anesthetize her internal pain. Later, she graduated to snorting heroin.

She further clouded her life by making regular trips to all three of Detroit's gambling casinos. Soon the economic peril she put herself into with gambling debt fueled the drinking and drugs. Nurses make good salaries at top hospitals, but alcohol, drugs, and gambling are an equation that ends in zero-sum reality. Over the weeks of getting to know Linda, she often told us that she had no family support in the Detroit area. She fell short of sharing with us how she got to be "totally without family," but we could see the loneliness in her eyes and the depression in her demeanor. Her trafficker was her drug dealer, and while he had not gained full control of Linda, he was clearly paving the way for her full dependence on him. She had not fully reconciled her sex work to her moral compass yet required it to fuel her drug addiction. She clung to us when we met her on the street, and we would have to eventually pull away so we could visit with our other friends on Monday nights. Within just a few weeks of meeting us, she had decided to let us help her. With our assistance, she was admitted to a local detox facility to begin the hard work toward sobriety and long-term rehabilitation. Our prayers went with her that she would get back to the plan and purpose that God had for her life.

VICTIM OF OPPORTUNITY

Tanya was the second nurse that we got to know in an unusual way. So many times, people that we talk to about human trafficking in our awareness sessions out in the community have a story about how they believe trafficking occurs. They imagine the frightening scenario of someone pulling up in a white windowless panel van, men jumping out, pulling an attractive female into the back of the van, closing the doors, handcuffing her to the floor of the van, whisking her off to some remote location where she gets put into a large dog cage, then put on a boat to South America. We tell people that that story hardly ever happens. Most of the many thousands of victims we have met didn't get introduced to trafficking in that Hollywood-scripted movie method. But we have learned that there are always exceptions to the rule. Tanya was a nurse scooped up by a trafficker in exactly that way.

Tanya was a thirty-something-year-old Black female with a vibrant smile and a petite figure. Despite her drug addiction, she seemed to be in excellent health, and her make-up and hair seemed perfect. Tanya was a traveling nurse who worked all over the United States with FEMA as well as nonprofit NGOs (non-governmental organizations), such as Samaritan's Purse. She would fly in and treat patients during emergencies or disasters such as a fire, flood, earthquake, or other forms of disaster.

Tanya had a drug addiction and found that working in these situations gave her the greatest possibility of hiding her drug dependency from her employers. Tanya had developed her dependency while partying fresh out of college with other kids who were experimenting with hard drugs. Tanya's problem was that she had the ability to secure drugs through nefarious means in the healthcare setting in which she worked. She would skim from the medications intended for patients that she was treating as she gave them half of their dose. She typically targeted patients who didn't want to take their drugs; they were unwittingly helping in her effort to sequester drugs for her own use. Tanya was pretty good at managing her addiction and continued skimming and using drugs like this for many years. She was able to walk an incredible tightrope for a long period of time. Nurses were in such demand at that time that few employers required that employees submit to random testing. Prestigious hospitals and healthcare facilities were only drug-testing new hires. Nurses' unions were fighting random drug testing in their profession. But Tanya continued dodging the bullet of getting caught and losing her license.

Tanya's family was in Detroit where she was living alone and resting between her assignments—sometimes for several weeks at a time. One late night, she stopped at a gas station here in the city, and a white windowless panel van pulled up next to her at the pump. Two men got out, quickly scooped her up, and put her in the back of the van. They had masks on their faces and said nothing to her. They didn't handcuff her, but they tied her legs and wrists together and covered her eyes with a blindfold. Tanya got a break that night when the van was involved in a traffic accident on a side street in Detroit. She realized that the people perpetrating the crime were most certainly intending to traffic her. She will never really know for sure, but that was her assessment at the time.

Tanya broke free from the van and called 911. The Detroit Police attempted to get her assistance through the National Human Trafficking Hotline. The hotline found her a bed in a home that helped victims of domestic violence but did not provide aid to trafficking victims. The first night that Tanya spent in this home, she began to feel the pangs of withdrawal from the drugs that her body so strongly craved, and she knew that she had to find another kind of help. The people at the domestic violence center were ill-equipped to help her, so she searched on her own and found our Night Angels hotline and called us.

We spoke with her and within the hour met her near the place she was staying. We quickly concluded that she needed to get to drug detox and long-term drug rehabilitation (which almost all our friends need when we meet them). From her story, we also concluded that she was a victim of trafficking (albeit short-lived) and needed detox services. Night Angels helped her get into detox, and over the next several days, we were able to get her to a long-term, Christian-based, in-patient drug rehabilitation program in southeastern Michigan. Tanya flourished in this environment. We believe that she found Jesus Christ again—she reaffirmed her beliefs from the time in her youth that she had committed her life to Jesus. After many months at this wonderful center, she struck out on her own and returned to the profession that she loved—nursing.

Despite that brush with the traffickers at the gas station and the shaking of her soul, Tanya broke her sobriety and returned to drugs after several months.

Thankfully, that wasn't the end of her story. Tanya went to another drug rehabilitation center on her own. She stayed in touch with our team for a few years of her journey. She has a sweet spirit, and we still pray for her and believe that the Lord has given her the strength to sustain her sobriety.

No One Is Immune

The idea that human trafficking exists only outside of the United States or primarily in developing countries is simply not true. When we learned about the real-life experiences of people in our own communities who had fallen victim to the insidious monster of human trafficking, we knew we could not ignore their pain and suffering.

A good education, stable job, decent income, good family, friends, and even church affiliation doesn't guarantee protection from a cunning trafficker.

This monster is insatiable. It hunts the people from every walk of life—people we love. In our work with Night Angels, we witnessed the treachery of sex trafficking being perpetrated against every gender, race, and ethnicity. We saw from stories like those of Linda and Tanya that no one is beyond this monster's reach. A good education, stable job, decent income, good family, friends, and even church affiliation doesn't guarantee protection from a cunning trafficker.

The thief comes only to steal and kill and destroy; I have come that they may have life, and have it to the full.
　　　　　　　　　　　　　　　　　　　　　—John 10:10

TINA

It was another dark, early spring night—it seems as if every Monday night for Night Angels is dark until we get into the month of May. In Michigan, if it is above freezing, we think that it is balmy, that Spring has come, and it is time to break out our shorts. We were a long way from opening day for the Detroit Tigers, so nothing was further from the truth. It was still just forty degrees outside. The four people inside our SUV were warm since we had started out that evening in our winter coats.

The team had been busy that evening. We had fed and given hygiene kits to almost thirty-five people. We minister to the homeless on the streets as well as trafficking victims, and we don't want to create friction between the two groups. Tonight, we also ministered to a former trafficker, Tony. Tony was well-known on the street, and he had become a friend of a different sort to us. Tony's grandfather had been a trafficker, and his father had been a trafficker. It was a family business. Tony had often prayed with us and received Jesus Christ as his Savior. He decided to leave the trafficking of girls behind. It was truly a miracle which only the Holy Spirit can accomplish.

Tony was a tall, thin Black man who was about six feet tall and looked far more aged than his fifty-six years. He lived in a dilapidated house by himself with too many cats to count. The paint was chipped, the windows had been covered with plywood to keep the cold air out, and the front door was hanging by just one hinge. The property was secured by a tall cyclone fence that was leaning terribly toward the road about three feet from its original location, and the gate had long been removed. It was a busy house, with the women he trafficked coming in and out and the men who dated them appearing at all hours of the day and night over the years.

After he had given his heart to the Lord, though, Tony began working as a legitimate house painter. He gave up all his sex-trafficking activities. He cleared the girls out of his house, put a coat of yellow paint on the outside, and locked his front door properly so that no strange men could come and go any longer. Tony remained living in the neighborhood where he had become so comfortable, as it was home to him and his cats. After his born-again experience, he met a nice woman and began a romantic relationship. She was from the local church that he was now attending, and her influence helped further strengthen Tony's faith.

Tony usually had lots to share. But this night, we needed to limit our time with him, as we had just spotted three women at the nearby corner. All three of the women had been under his control at some time in their life on the streets. We always affirmed Tony for his brave change of lifestyle. We offered to pray with him and blessed him with one of our lunches, plus an extra lunch, so he could take it to work with him the next day.

We made our way to the corner where the women were laughing and talking. Our friends are usually bundled up and fighting the cold this time of year, but all three of these women had their jackets unbuttoned to reveal some skin. We pulled the SUV up and offered them a free lunch and a hygiene kit. The three women engaged in conversation with our team almost simultaneously. One of them was Tina.

Remarkably healthy looking, Tina was about five foot, five inches tall, thin but not terribly underweight. She was about forty years old with long, jet-black hair, a fair complexion, and unforgettable green eyes. Tina was eager to talk; in fact, she was eager to leave her trafficker. She agreed right then to allow our team to execute a rescue plan and take her to detox.

The Lord cleared our path, and on the way to detox that night, Tina began to tell us her story—a story that continued to unfold as we mentored her through the next several years of her life. Tina spent four days in detox and then moved to a long-term Christian-based drug rehabilitation program in the Detroit area. She progressed through the various stages of sobriety, determined to get her life back to the plan and purpose God had for her.

Tina truly began a new life with our team that *balmy* forty-degree night on a dark street in Detroit.

THE PARTY LIFE

Tina was an average kid in high school, coming from a good family. She was athletic but didn't go out for sports. She liked to sing but never tried the choral group at school. She was always the life of the party, and people loved her for that. Tina had begun smoking marijuana in high school like most of the kids in her social circle. *What harm could that do?* she thought. Her high school boyfriend, Jake, was also a marijuana smoker.

Both Tina and Jake had good relationships with their families. Neither had plans to go to college, assuming that their success at the part-time jobs they'd had in high school would carry over to better jobs and ultimately a good life. Tina was attractive and friendly and could always get hired and earn decent tips as a waitress. Jake was mechanically inclined. He knew he could fix almost anything, including cars, and wasn't worried about his job prospects. The world was their oyster, and although they both thought they would get married when the time was right, they weren't in a hurry. They had the rest of their lives to do the adult thing. Their first priority was partying, and party they did.

Tina's lifestyle troubled her parents. They constantly badgered her about coming home late, even on weekday nights. Her parents never saw her on the weekends, as some of her parties lasted for days on end. Tina was less interested in her work habits and more interested in her social status—not only with her former high school friends, but also with her adult friends whom her parents had never met. Her parents did not approve of these new friends that seemed to lack the scruples they had taught Tina.

Tina's parents had initially liked Jake, but he, too, seemed to be coming apart at the seams and on the same destructive path as Tina. The two fed off each other, trying to see which one of them would be the most extolled as the life of the party at any time and in any situation. The young couple made less and less time for family gatherings like birthday parties, Christmas, and Easter celebrations. Tina drifted further and further from her safety net.

Tina scuffled with the police during her nineteenth year. First, there was a minor fender bender with her parents' car. She got a ticket for driving impaired but admitted she should have been given a DUI. The second offense was a loitering charge for being inside a place where drugs were being sold. Since she wasn't in possession of any drugs, she dismissed the charges to her parents as "no big deal."

Her concerning behavior continued. Then, one morning, her parents couldn't wake her up to go to work. They didn't know if she was out cold due to alcohol or drugs (or both), but the turmoil and worry they had endured had reached a breaking point. They told her she needed to move out and get her own place. They had hoped that kicking Tina out of the house at age twenty would deter her from this dangerous road she was following, but it didn't.

Tina and Jake decided to pool their money and get a place together. Between his job as an automobile mechanic and her flirtatious waitressing skills, they had enough to cover rent and buy a used car that was stylish enough to get them to and from their endless party venues.

While other couples their age were finishing school, saving for a house, pursuing a hobby, or traveling, Tina and Jake were always looking for a good time and the next party. Their constant search for more adrenaline and excitement led them into a crowd that experimented with drugs much harder than marijuana, and their own drug use escalated.

Tina and Jake tried a potpourri of drugs that produced a variety of physiological and psychogenic effects. Cocaine became their favorite. They felt that they could control themselves better with cocaine and have some semblance of a normal life. Cocaine allowed them to walk a tightrope and continue to work. It seemed to have fewer side effects and less visible physical evidence on the body. Their coworkers and family members noticed fewer tell-tale signs of what they were doing or how deep their addiction was taking them. For ten years, Tina and Jake walked this tight rope, drinking, partying, snorting cocaine, but still managing to hold life together.

The wheels came off when they were introduced to speedballs. A speedball is a polydrug that combines a stimulant with a depressant, usually an opioid, which may be taken intravenously or by nasal inhaling. The most common mixture for speedballs is cocaine and heroin; however, amphetamines can also be combined with morphine or fentanyl. What started as an occasional speedball turned into a regular speedball, and then a steady diet.

Before they knew it, Tina and Jake were in their thirties with little to nothing to show for their life or work. They had gotten married, but the drugs were beginning to affect not only their health but also their outlook on life. Their sustained cocaine use, along with the speedballs, caused both to have difficulties on their jobs. Jake especially had run-ins with his boss and his coworkers over the most trivial of things. Jake didn't have problems with just one but several employers over a multi-year period. The problems on these jobs had put him in a tough spot. Employers had begun doing pre-employment drug screens for hiring, and some were doing random drug testing. Jake knew he couldn't pass a drug test, so he had to take lesser-paying jobs where employers didn't screen for drugs. Most of the time, Jake was being paid under the table as a ghost employee. Eventually, he was unable to get any work because of his drug habit.

Tina had a decent job, and although she, too, was having the same drug-test problem, she was able to stay employed. She just had to wear more provocative clothing to keep the patrons happy at the bars and restaurants where she worked. And she, too, was usually paid off the books by employers who were less inclined to follow the rules. The fuse finally ran out on Tina when her drug habit kept her from showing up on time, and she was unable to put in a full day's work for a full day's pay. The couple was unemployed, and they knew they couldn't go to their families for financial support since they had deliberately abandoned them during this heavy partying period of their lives.

'NO SEX INVOLVED'

Jake had an idea, one that probably wasn't his own since he was in a drug-induced fog most of the time. He had found an ad in the local underground newspaper for women who were interested in getting paid to date men. The ad said, "No sex involved."

He talked Tina into giving it a try.

Although he refused to admit that he knew it was a scam, Jake knew the dating service was designed to hook up women for the purpose of commercial sex. He believed that if he got Tina sufficiently high before the date, she would be able to pull it off. Using all of his charms on her, he convinced his wife that she only needed to go on enough dates to pay the rent and support their drug addictions. Tina agreed to go on the first date, and then another, and the couple realized she was good at sex work.

> He transitioned from
> husband to her manager,
> then simply to her trafficker.

Jake's manipulation of Tina went into high gear. He transitioned from husband to her manager, then simply to her trafficker. Customers could leave reviews in the underground newspaper. Initially, Jake gladly provided fake reviews to increase Tina's clientele. He also convinced her to get breast implants to improve her marketability and earning potential. If she got a bad review from a customer, Jake became enraged. If another girl got a super review for performing a sexual act that Tina wouldn't or couldn't, Jake would blow up at her.

Jake's temperament changed. He no longer had a job, so his only focus was managing Tina so that he could get the drugs that had become his god. Jake's abuse of Tina was escalating, and he beat her several times during his speedball-driven outbursts. The abuse did not mark Tina too badly on the outside, but it scarred her on the inside.

Age and drugs took their toll on Tina's looks as she approached her late thirties. She couldn't compete with the twenty-year-old girls who were getting posted in the underground newspaper. So Jake pushed her into going out to the street to do sex work on the avenue where we eventually met her during our Night Angels outreach.

Tina had grown weary of Jake's abuse and control. He had morphed from her high school sweetheart to her lover and husband, but now he was simply her pimp. He controlled every move and questioned every action: Where was she? How long was she there? Whom did she see? What sex acts did she perform? Couldn't she have charged more? Couldn't she talk the "John" into spending more money? Jake's questions were endless. He constantly badgered her to bring in more money—and abused her if the nightly cash deposit wasn't up to his demands. As always, he was careful not to leave too many physical marks, but his emotional abuse cut to her core.

That spring night when we met Tina, she was absolutely disgusted with Jake. While she was standing on the corner with her friends, he and his buddies were planning a burglary they thought would be an easy score. Tina had finally realized that Jake had changed. She was revolted by his abuse and the person he had become, but even then, she couldn't bring herself to call him a trafficker.

A NEW LIFE

In the rehabilitation program, Tina's physical and mental health stabilized. She flourished when she found the Lord, and her relationship with Him grew.

The stronger and healthier she got mentally, physically, and spiritually, the more clearly she was able to think about what she had been through. She thought through all of Jake's abuse, his trickery, his manipulation, and his evil intent, and she realized that she had, in fact, been trafficked by someone she had once loved. She chose to divorce Jake.

Tina's health stabilized, and her relationship with the Lord grew stronger. Several years later, however, she relapsed into drug use for a short period. Fortunately, she chose to restart her walk back to sobriety.

She got married a second time and moved out of Michigan. This second husband insisted that what she needed was a peaceful mountainous environment in which to heal. He happily moved her to his secluded cabin in Kentucky where he began to abuse her almost immediately. Although she was trapped in that secluded cabin and the surrounding wooded mountains for months before breaking free of him, she was stronger mentally and spiritually than she had ever been before. She managed to escape to a safe house and called to let us know of her whereabouts. She was free once again.

Most people would think a scenario like Jake and Tina's is atypical; unfortunately, it is all too common for a husband and wife to be tangled in trafficking together. Tina wisely continues to seek emotional support and mental health services to heal from the trauma she endured in what should have been a loving relationship. We continue to pray for her strength as she becomes who God created her to be.

Therefore, if anyone is in Christ, the new creation has come: The old has gone, the new is here!
—*2 Corinthians 5:17*

A Transcending Approach

Transgender issues, gay rights, and relationship issues that fall outside the traditional biblical model of Christian marriage are the topic of hot debate. In others, some church circles, for instance, these topics are avoided at all costs. Pastors who pray for the lost often do so while secretly hoping that no one *different* shows up at the sanctuary door in search of prayer and healing. The stress of having to deal with the issues or confrontations that might occur within their congregation seem overwhelming. Church leaders sit on the sidelines of the social justice battlefield while the right and left wings fight. No legislative body, executive authority, or church governing boards seems to *win*.

Many people with stronger voices than ours have spent multiple hours on air and in print analyzing this issue, but suffice it to say there is a whirlwind, socially, politically, and within the Church, about how people should be treated who live in the gay or transgender community. Churches continue to argue about whether gay and transgender people should be allowed to attend their church, much less become members. Then there's the Pandora's box of related questions: Can they participate in sacraments such as baptism, communion, and marriage?

We talked about these issues with our Night Angels team members many times. In these discussions, we learned that despite the diversity of our team's church backgrounds, most came from churches that would not easily welcome gay or transgender folks into their church community. Some might show them to the door immediately. Others might be a little less confrontational, but welcoming? No. This realization challenged all of us to do some soul-searching about how we should show the love of Christ to our gay, transvestite, or transgender friends on the street.

> We were going to show the love of Christ to everyone—without bias, without condescension, without coming to conclusions about how or why they came to their lifestyle.

From our very first outreach night, we understood that we had to decide what kind of ministry we were going to be. Our Night Angels team immediately saw, and would continue to see, gay, transgender, and transvestite individuals on any given Monday night. This wasn't something we could avoid. Nor did we want to. We decided from the onset that our team was going to put away all our biases coming into the ministry. We committed to loving whomever we met. We were going to minister to and pray with them. We were going to show the love of Christ to everyone— without bias, without condescension, without coming to conclusions about how or why they came to their lifestyle. We would hold hands with and hug all our friends, and if anyone couldn't do that, then they couldn't be part of our team. Few failed to meet that standard over our years of working on the street.

LOVE FIRST

During our discussions with our team, one person shared a story from his childhood. He had been hospitalized and shared a semi-private room with someone he thought was a little boy about his age—seven years old.

He was much sicker than the other little boy, but both were in the hospital for a couple of weeks together. The two talked, colored together, played board games, and became good friends. Years later, our team member's parents told him that the little boy who had been his roommate in the hospital had been born with both male and female genitalia. During his stay, the doctors completed a host of genetic tests on this child and performed a kind of gender-assignment surgery on him. Our team member still wonders: Did the little boy become comfortable with being a man? What pronouns did he use? Did he get married? Did he have children? Where did his future take him? That little boy's story continues to affect the way our team member processes gender-related issues.

As our team member spoke, we were all convicted of the truth that the Christian Church must find a way to love all of our friends on the street. We prayed that our team would be bold in taking the first step toward showing our friends what the love of Christ is like. Perhaps if they had been turned off by the Church in the past, by our sharing that Christ still loved them, these hurting individuals could find the Lord in and around our SUV.

MALCOMB

Malcomb was one of the first gay friends we met on the street who was dressed as a woman. He was born a male and asked us to refer to him as Malcomb, even though he was known on the street as Marilyn. The first night we saw him, he was wearing a tight red spandex dress and high heels. This is uncommon dress for our female friends on the street, but common dress for a man transitioning and wanting to be seen as the "Pretty Woman." He told us that he was gay and desired to become a woman, but that he had no intention of going through the medical treatments and surgeries necessary to redefine his gender.

Malcomb hung out at a gay nightclub in our neighborhood and wore women's clothing most of the time. He told us that gay men on the street make more money than their female counterparts for sex work. Malcomb lived in a combination drug house/ bordello run by a straight (heterosexual) woman, but he was being trafficked by a gay man in the neighborhood. Malcomb paid rent to the woman so he could sleep at the house at night but picked men up either on the street or at the nightclub that he had made his pseudo headquarters. He would engage in sex near the night-club in the date's car or in a nearby public park. Rarely did he frequent a motel in the area.

Malcomb was difficult to minister to because he had such a hard exterior. He had followed Jesus as a young man but had turned away from his faith through the years. Over time he began to trust us enough to talk about his background. He always seemed a little entitled. If we had coats or clothing to give out that night, he was always particular about what color or size the clothing might be. That common attitude was always baffling to our team. It would seem that someone living in such an environment as brutal as a

Michigan winter might not be so particular. After all, if you are nearing frostbite, does it matter what color the coat is that someone is trying to give you? To Malcomb, it did. He even exerted his entitled behavior so aggressively one cold winter's night that he sweet-talked one of our team members right out of his new pair of North Face winter gloves. It was a lesson that team member never forgot: Do not let our friends become bullies.

We had only ministered to Malcomb for a short period of time when we learned that he had become the victim of a hate crime. The story in the neighborhood was that Malcomb was picked up in a car with a date when he was dressed as a woman, and when the date realized that Marilyn had male genitalia, he killed him and left him lying face up in the street. Initially, we heard of his death and then ultimately got an official confirmation of this story. Malcomb's murder was the first time we knew about a hate crime perpetrated against one of our friends, but it would certainly not be the last. In our ten years of outreach, we saw our gay, transgender, and transvestite friends murdered, maimed, and mistreated many times.

One week after Malcomb's death, the neighborhood held a memorial service at the site where his body was found. A member of our team attended the memorial and witnessed the mourners as they considered the grim reality of the evil that surrounded them and that they, too, could easily suffer a similar end. Many tears were shed as news of his death reverberated through the grapevine we had come to know so well. Our friends knew that Malcomb wasn't an exception but rather a rule on the street.

ALFREDO / MERCADA

Alfredo was a man who had chosen to live as a woman and had taken the street name of Mercada. She had grown up in the Church and had a vast knowledge of biblical truth. But the scriptural truths that she could recite quite clearly seemed to have been lost somehow and somewhere. She wasn't following the Lord and was in a dark place in her life.

Mercada had a cold exterior that had been hardened beyond her years on the street. Her dark skin seemed to glisten in the night light from a heavy makeup foundation that made her look quite stunning. Her long straight black wigs were always coiffed perfectly and her nails were immaculate. She was clearly an intravenous drug user, but she seemed to have the ability to manage her addiction enough to show that she was in control. She was a leader of sorts on the street, and over the years, she not only did sex work to support her habit but she ran drug houses for drug dealers and took on the role known on the street as a bottom b*tch. In this role, she played the middleman in the world of human trafficking. In return, she secured (however tenuously) a better place to stay, more drugs, or general favor with the bad guys at the expense of other trafficking victims. Mercada would come and pray with our team regularly and take a hygiene kit and a lunch. She, too, had a great sense of entitlement, asking us to deliver her food to the second floor of a drug house where she lived. We generally refused that request, but occasionally relented if we had an abundance of food.

After years of our praying with Mercada and trying to build trust, she allowed us to help her get off the streets. The problem quickly intensified as detox facilities and long-term drug rehabilitation programs in the Detroit area did not (at the time) permit transvestite, transgender, or gay individuals to cross dress. To enter a treatment program, Mercada would have to resume the role of the male, Alfredo. The drug rehabilitation facility where we took Alfredo specialized in treating gay, transvestite, and transgender individuals—despite the fact that they required all residents to dress and use pronouns of their birth gender. Alfredo was generally successful in this drug rehabilitation program but relapsed and ended up back on the street performing sex work dressed as a woman. Quickly after Mercada's relapse, she was involved in a crime in which a gun was used and was put in prison for several years. Mercada is now out of prison and living in another state.

TONI

Toni was one of the kindest friends that our team had ever met on the street. Toni was born a man, grew up as a man, but knew from a young age that he was gay and wanted to transition to being a woman. Toni had even begun the process of gender reassignment surgery, was taking hormone therapy, and had undergone breast implant surgery.

Toni was tall and seemed imposing as a woman because of her height, but she was so kind and charismatic that she never seemed to overwhelm our team. She always prayed with us and loved to talk with us during outreach times. Our team was never sure of the status of her gender-reassignment surgery, but she could easily pass as a woman, looking feminine in short dresses and tight-fitting clothing. Toni was working under Mercada, performing sex work on the streets. But one night in the neighborhood, Toni was working on the street late. Someone driving by decided, for no apparent reason, to take a shot at Toni. Toni saw the gun appear from the car window as it was passing by. She tried to turn away from the shooter, but the bullet pierced her lower back. She was quickly transported to Detroit's Receiving Hospital by EMS.

Some of our team members went to visit Toni in the hospital after the shooting. She was provided with what we understood to be a medical detoxification from her addiction to drugs. Other drugs were used in an intravenous infusion, allowing her body to detox while being sedated. Toni's wound was life threatening, but she survived. The bullet, however, had injured her spinal cord and several vertebrae in her back, and she will forever use a wheelchair. When we visited Toni in the hospital, she was her usual jovial self and was incredibly positive about her future. She told us that her family was permitting her to return home to recuperate. The fact that she was no longer addicted was a positive aspect for her to be able to reconnect with her family. It was unclear to our team how she would proceed with her gender-reassignment surgery. The most important aspect of her story is that she gave God all the glory for having survived the shooting, and she knew that her life had been spared for a purpose in His kingdom.

As we stated earlier in this chapter, it was our team's intent to be the Lord's first line of outreach to show the love of Christ to all of our friends on the streets. The Church has promulgated a long list of traditions that serve to shun, ostracize, and push out our friends—particularly those who are gay and transgender—who have been victims of human trafficking.

Therefore, we call upon the Church, pastors, church leadership, and congregants worldwide to consider embracing the need to reinforce the example of love that Christ shows to all of us. Let us initiate the conversation and welcome all those who may enter the sanctuary doors. It will take a large dose of Christ's love to over-come the pain of the traffickers and those who have perpetrated hate crimes against this group of our friends. Their pain is real, and the world has no answer for them. There isn't enough psychoanal-ysis, medication, and trauma-based therapy to heal them, but the Lord can, if we are prepared to be His hands and feet.

While Jesus was having dinner at Matthew's house, many tax collectors and sinners came and ate with him and his disciples. When the Pharisees saw this, they asked his disciples, "Why does your teacher eat with tax collectors and sinners?"

On hearing this, Jesus said, "It is not the healthy who need a doctor, but the sick. But go and learn what this means: 'I desire mercy, not sacrifice.' For I have not come to call the righteous, but sinners."

—*Matthew 9:10–13*

CINDI

Harsh. That's how our Night Angels team members often described the streets during outreach. The harshness felt almost palpable. It is hard to define or to adequately describe. In the winter, it always seemed colder on the street. When it snowed, the flakes seemed bigger, the snow seemed deeper, and the ice made the roads more treacherous than those in our comfortable suburbs. In the summer, it seemed hotter, and the humidity seemed higher. Any smells were made more pungent. When we heard the backfire of a car, it was loud. Dogs were dirtier—skinny, malnourished, and badly in need of care and grooming.

The roads in the city needed snowplowing in the winter and street sweeping in the summer. Every structure we saw in our outreach neighborhood needed a coat of paint. Streetlights or storefront lights were usually out. Homes on every block we passed needed maintenance, bordering on the uninhabitable. Smiles on people walking on the street were almost nonexistent. Children never played with the joy that children should. People's clothing was tattered and ill-fitting. Little attention was paid to style or the latest fashion. Even on a sunny day, the neighborhood had a grayness that couldn't be brightened.

Was this a bias on our part because we were outsiders to the community? Was it because we were fearful of the danger that lurked at every turn in the road, at every doorway, at every traffic light? Our team didn't know the answers, but we saw all this grittiness in the faces of our friends and heard it in their voices. Was it fear that we saw in their eyes? Did their callousness come from hate? Were they mean-spirited because they had been up for twenty-four, thirty-six, forty-eight hours on a heroin high? Could they not talk because they had just been beaten by their trafficker because they had not returned enough money from their last date with a John? Had they just fought with one of their fellow sex workers on the street who "ripped them off" over some financial issue regarding a deck of heroin? Even after ten years of street ministry, we couldn't fully understand the harshness we saw and felt on the street.

PRAYING INTO THE DARKNESS

Whenever we pulled over in our SUV to ask our friends if they wanted a lunch and a hygiene kit, we knew the general dynamics on the street and the danger in which we were operating. But we never knew the mental and emotional state of the friend that we would be approaching. Cindi was a friend that we saw regularly on the street, and she didn't take well to interacting with us for several months after we first met her. Cindi was slightly built, and her bleach-blonde hair wasn't covering her brown roots. The black lipstick, heavy dark eye makeup, and black leather collar with studs added an edge to her already harsh exterior. There was always callousness in her voice and her behaviors when around us. She often crossed the street to avoid us.

Despite her lack of interest in our lunches and hygiene kits, clothing, and prayer, we were relentless in our attempts to insert the love of Jesus between her and her trafficker. Eventually, after a spell of cold nights, we could see the hunger in her eyes, and Cindi accepted a lunch, a hygiene kit, and some warm clothing. Following that first breakthrough, she listened to what we had to say, and we told her about our offer to help get her out of the neighborhood and into a Christian-based restorative care program. Week after week we gave her another one of our business cards which had our twenty-four-hour hotline number on it. Each time she would tuck it into her bra "for safe keeping." We begged her, week after week, to call us and let us help her.

But we never got the call.

The last time we saw Cindi on the street, she probably weighed less than 100 pounds, and her long brown hair had become extremely thin and tangled. It was during the dead cold of winter in Michigan, and she wore jeans that were full of holes and was without a warm coat. Abscesses on her arms and face showed the signs of where she had been shooting up heroin with dirty needles. Cindi had made an indelible mark on our team. We cared for her so much and believed God had a better plan and purpose for her life that didn't involve her present environment or circumstances.

Several weeks of not seeing Cindi turned into several months. Each outreach, our team worried about not seeing her and would collectively pray for her in her absence. We remembered the severity of Cindi's countenance. She never smiled, she never said a kind word, we never heard her laugh or tell a joke. Despite all the efforts that our team members employed, we were never able to draw her out and find a subject matter or a softness with which to connect. None of us ever seemed to crash through her hardened exterior despite sharing with her the love of Christ. There was a rumor on the street after we no longer continued to see her that she was pregnant, but we had seen no evidence of a pregnancy. By this time, it was winter, and heavy clothing may have covered up a small baby bump, but we had no way of being sure about the pregnancy or to where she had disappeared. We prayed that, somehow, she had found her way out of the chaos, drugs, and sex work.

NO TURNING BACK

Some months later, members of our team were visiting the Christian-based restorative care center we preferred, when Cindi ran up and embraced them in a hug. She had remembered the name of the center to which we had begged her to let us take her. One day she just decided to go. She had found her *own* way to the center! Our team members hugged her back, absolutely thrilled to see her there and *smiling*.

Part of our mission with Night Angels was advocacy. As much as our friends wanted and allowed us to, we would walk beside them during their drug recovery. Upon reconnecting with Cindi, our team sought to support and mentor her. Women from our team met with her monthly for activities and conversations and, over time, the relationships they shared became deep friendships.

> As much as our friends wanted and
> allowed us to, we would walk beside
> them during their drug recovery.

It wasn't long before Cindi began to share parts of her story with us. She told us that her mother and father had divorced when she was in elementary school. Cindi continued to have a good relationship with her parents, even after the divorce. She had begun using marijuana at twelve, and it became a gateway for her to graduate to the harder and more addictive drugs, crack cocaine, and heroin. Her need for heroin outpaced her addiction to crack cocaine. She got involved with gangs and drug dealers who were also engaged in human trafficking. It was first one gang and then later various drug dealers who exploited her for sex work. She ended up being trafficked by several gangs and traffickers for over ten years.

She lived with a group of girls in a house that we knew to be nefarious. It was situated on the corner of a street not very far from the home of the mayor of Detroit. The rat-infested house had been condemned many years previously, classified as blight and slated to be torn down by the city. Our team had heard about this house and the evil activities there. We avoided it during our outreach route because we knew that getting too close could put our team in harm's way. Even so, we saw numerous vehicles come and go from this location, including various delivery trucks that parked at the site for long periods. The girls living in this house seemed hard core, even by Cindi's standards. They were known for their tough attitude with clients and their expensive prices. We didn't know that the harshness that we had seen in Cindi was actually her marketing tool.

Cindi found out she was pregnant while she was serving time in Wayne County Jail. She had been arrested for prostitution and possession of drug paraphernalia, and it was in jail that her body started detoxing. Heroin detox is difficult, and detoxing in jail is difficult and ugly. Usually, the addicted person lies on the cell floor near a floor drain that catches the vomit. She may stay in that position for two days while her body heaves and coughs. Pain wracks every fiber of her body as the drugs leave. From the stories we have heard about detoxing in jail, the authorities do little to facilitate the inmates during the process.

Cindi had also been addicted to crack cocaine. Crack doesn't necessarily require detoxing, but it doesn't make the detox from heroin any easier. Cindi had also been a longtime user of marijuana, so her first few weeks in that jail cell were a torture indescribable to anyone who hasn't been through it.

After going through that hell on the jail floor, Cindi made up her mind that she wasn't going to return to the life on the street from whence she had come. She made a commitment to herself to get her act together for the baby's sake and to raise the baby while making herself into a mother. Her daughter, Hope, was born while she was housed in the jail and, fortunately for her, her awesome mother and stepfather took the baby and raised it while Cindi finished her stint in jail. Upon her release, she voluntarily went to restorative care in Pontiac, Michigan, a place where she could get long-term rehabilitation and learn how to be a good mother with her child at her side. The beauty of this center is that it is focused on Christ. There, Cindi received a major infusion of help from the Holy Spirit.

Cindi spent the next three years at the center. She flourished there, worked on her relationship with the Lord, and stayed on track with her sobriety. While there, she met Rick, who was also in the program. She often saw him at church and knew he had two daughters from a previous marriage. Cindi and Rick were attracted to one another but agreed to follow the rules of the program, dating only while supervised. When he completed the two-year program, Rick moved into a mobile home so that he could create a more permanent lifestyle for himself and have a place for visitation days with his daughters. All the while, he was hopeful to one day make a home for Cindi and Hope.

With both of them holding well-paying managerial jobs in the community, Cindi moved in with Rick to a subsidized apartment nearby. They struggled with the fact that they were living together and not following the biblical teachings they had learned, so six months later, they decided to get married.

Sometime later, Cindi and Rick invited members of our Night Angels team to celebrate another new beginning: They were having a baby. Cindi and Rick were blessed with a beautiful baby boy. They are wonderful parents to Hope, who is now in kindergarten, and they have moved into a larger, two-bedroom apartment that accommodates all the children when Rick's two daughters come to visit. They attend a local church together, continue to enjoy their jobs, and they have great relationships with Rick's former wife as well as Cindi's parents.

> Our team was blessed to know Cindi.
> The evolution and sanctification
> of her faith was a beautiful
> miracle to witness.

Our team was blessed to know Cindi. The evolution and sanctification of her faith was a beautiful miracle to witness. Today, Cindi's former hard and coarse countenance have been replaced by the light and image of Christ that exudes from her and her family. Her story is truly incredible. The Lord absolutely had a plan and purpose for her life, and she is living it.

Such stories of success gave us the courage to keep going back to the streets, no matter how harsh the environment or the people. We learned to trust the Lord and follow His leading, trusting that

He was always working His will, regardless of how things appeared in the moment.

> I planted the seed, Apollos watered it, but God has been making it grow. So neither the one who plants nor the one who waters is anything, but only God, who makes things grow. The one who plants and the one who waters have one purpose, and they will each be rewarded according to their own labor. For we are co-workers in God's service; you are God's field, God's building.
> —*1 Corinthians 3:6–9*

WHAT NOW?

It has been difficult to relive our years on the street as we have described the people we have come to know and love. We felt it was God who led us to our work, and it is God who is now leading us to share our experiences in this book.

Knowing that we are doing what we are called to do doesn't necessarily make it easy. It doesn't make the pain of loss and disappointment and heartache go away. This process, however, has reminded us of the many blessings we experienced by watching God at work in so many people's lives—including our own.

When we launched the Night Angels ministry in 2016, our action plan was awareness, assistance, advocacy, and apostleship. This book is largely focused on awareness. We wanted to communicate the evil reality that sex trafficking is happening across this nation to our daughters and sons, neighbors, friends, and family members. It happens every minute of every day. It exists in every part of our cities and towns and is a hellish attack on society—on *humanity.*

You've read several times throughout this book that anyone can become a victim of human trafficking. That fact can sound desperate or depressing, but the good news is that awareness is one of the best weapons we have against this crime:

- Awareness that sex trafficking happens right where you live—in your community, city, and state

- Awareness of the things that make people most vulnerable

- Awareness of what it might look like if someone you know is being trafficked

- Awareness that Hollywood gets it wrong much of the time—it isn't sexy, glamorous, pretty, or exciting

- Awareness that prostitution, pornography, and drugs are inextricably linked to the crime of human trafficking

- Awareness that it is not okay to look the other way

We also want you to be aware on the most basic level of how you can help. If you see someone who you believe is being trafficked and is in imminent danger, you should call 911 to report it. You can also call the National Human Trafficking Hotline at (888) 373-7888 for assistance.

If you would like to make a financial contribution toward street outreach to human trafficking victims in the Detroit area, we have worked with and highly recommend Elli's House, an incredible organization led by Deb Ellinger. Elli's House is a 501(c)(3) non-profit organization serving homeless and runaway women involved in human trafficking in the city of Detroit. Their mission is to abolish sex trafficking in Detroit through building relationships, offering safe shelter, and providing education. They can be contacted through their website at ellishouse313.com.

HOW WILL YOU HELP?

We hope that as you've read our friends' stories, you have begun to wonder where you fit into the story and asked some big questions:

What can I do?

How can I help?

We started the Night Angels ministry with the intent that if we could help just one individual out of the world of trafficking, that would be enough to fuel our passion for ending this slavery. During our ten years, we touched over 7,000 lives and helped more than 600 people flee their traffickers.

But we didn't start there. We started by volunteering with another organization in our community that was ministering to sex trafficking victims in another part of the city.

Maybe you can do the same.

Maybe there is a shelter or church program or community outreach that could use someone just like you to pray, donate funds, or hand out meals and clothes.

You can easily share this book with others to help increase the level of awareness about sex trafficking for the people in your community, family, church, and circle of influence.

Or maybe you feel called to start an outreach ministry like Night Angels in your community. If so, we would love to pray for you and with you. You can reach us at twylabaggett@yahoo.com.

Regardless of how you choose to get involved, we know that your life will be forever changed by the decision to stand up for those who have no voice, for those who are hurting, marginalized, and lost.

We have shared stories like these with countless audiences across our city, the nation, and even internationally. After overcoming the disbelief that human trafficking happens everywhere, the next emotion that tends to overwhelm people is righteous indignation. The fact that anyone today is subjected to the kind of horrendous pain and suffering that our friends on the streets endure is shocking, offensive, and utterly appalling. We and our Night Angels team members have felt all those same emotions. It was that outrage and passion that moved us into action. We pray that will be true for you too.

PLEASE, DON'T LOOK THE OTHER WAY

At the end of awareness presentations, we often close with a quote from William Wilberforce: "Look the other way, but you can never again say that you did not know."

Wilberforce was a slave ship owner and slave trader who had a ferocious awakening to the power of the Holy Spirit. He turned away from his livelihood of transporting and selling slaves and gave his life to the Lord. It was through the power of his relationship with Jesus Christ that he became a member of the British Parliament and a powerful and staunch abolitionist. Wilberforce was instrumental in ending slavery in the British Empire in 1833, many years before Lincoln's Emancipation Proclamation became law in the United States. He also wrote "Amazing Grace," a hymn that has impacted generations of Christians ever since.

If Wilberforce could change the world by working in the British Parliament and penning the words of a song, you can join the fight against human trafficking and make a difference using your God-given talents right where you live. We also believe that the Church has a pivotal role in this effort and should be leading the way to abolish sex slavery in the world. Our government, social service agencies, and law enforcement have not been able to stem the tide of this insidious evil.

Martin Luther King said that if every pastor in every pulpit in the United States would stand for the cause of civil rights and turn the hearts of those in the Church, civil rights would become a reality. We believe that today the same holds true for human trafficking. If every pastor extolled Jesus as the ultimate example of social justice, human trafficking would be dealt a death blow.

He has shown you, O mortal, what is good.
And what does the Lord require of you?
To act justly and to love mercy
and to walk humbly with your God.

—Micah 6:8

Acknowledgments

The British poet John Donne told us that no man is an island . . . no man stands alone.[4] We have lived that truth. Here follows a list of those who stood with us through it all. We offer them our deepest gratitude.

Night Angels Team—We thank our diverse group of volunteers who were absolutely the best team that we could have assembled—it was truly the work of the Holy Spirit. The team bonded much like a family within itself. We went to the streets week after week in all types of weather and conditions. We were chased by pimps, drug dealers, and bad guys of all kinds. But our team's commitment to the mission in which we were engaged never faltered.

Night Angels Sponsors and Donors—We were blessed with sponsors that donated fully-packed, delicious lunches with snacks and healthy sandwiches that we could pass out each week. Our friends often told us they had not eaten all week when we handed them a fresh meal. These lunches were put together by individuals, families, small groups, churches, schools, educators, counselors, book clubs, survivors of human trafficking, and one-time donors. We never had to go on outreach empty-handed. Volunteers donated hand-made items, including blankets, scarves, hats, and holiday gifts. We also received gloves, socks, hand warmers, winter coats, and coats that turned into sleeping bags. Items that were donated were stored in either our rented storage facility or our own garage. Twyla would pack that SUV to the gills so that our friends had everything that we could possibly bless them with for the week. As rescue calls came into our 24/7 hotline, we gave these victims donated survivor back-packs with absolutely everything a person needs to be comfortable in a detox center, always in the correct size. Generous financial con-tributions were used to supplement our inventory when needed, to reimburse our drivers for their expenses, and occasionally to bless our "survivors" with an evening out with their mentors.

Rebecca Huey—We would like to thank our good friend and fam-ily member Rebecca for first enlightening us about the problem of human trafficking in the United States. If it were not for her passionate overture to us that spawned our own passion, we might never have taken steps to form Night Angels.

The Joseph Project—This wonderful network of attorneys helped our friends—pro bono—so many times to navigate themselves out of the myriads of legal issues they faced while emerging from the dark evil of trafficking.

Detroit Police Department (DPD) Special Victims Unit (SVU)—We thank you for taking a step out of the "norm" and welcoming Night Angels to share your circle. For seeing our friends with fresh eyes as victims of crimes and wanting a better life for them. For "having our backs" and keeping us safe on the streets and in the community.

Compassion Pregnancy Center—These wonderful professionals helped our friends, who might have been or were pregnant, with love and the greatest level of professionalism.

Donna McCauley—Thank you for being our own mentor and friend as well as a fellow prayer warrior for our friends on the street.

Linda Cadariu—We extend our sincerest thanks to this team member who was the initial editor of our book. We lived and wrote these stories, but you helped us communicate them in written form, for which we will be forever grateful.

Children—To our children, we say thank you for being on our team and supporting this work these many years, in so many capacities. Your love and devotion to the cause of fighting human trafficking kept us strong in our battle.

END NOTES

1 – Merriam-Webster.com. "Human Trafficking."
https://www.merriam-webster.com/dictionary/human%20trafficking.

2 – US Department of State. "About Human Trafficking."
https://2021-2025.state.gov/humantrafficking-about-human-trafficking.

3 – National Human Trafficking Hotline. "National Statistics."
https://humantraffickinghotline.org/en/statistics.

4 – Donne, John. *No Man Is an Island: Selected from the Writings of John Donne.*
United States: Random House, 1970.

About the Authors

Mel & Twyla Baggett have been married for more than fifty years. Mel retired as vice president of human resources for a large steel company, and Twyla retired as a physical education teacher at a Christian school. Together they formed a Christian anti-human trafficking ministry called Night Angels. Both Mel and Twyla and a team of about twenty-eight volunteers went out on the streets of Detroit attempting to locate, help, and assist women and men engaged in trafficking. In a total of over ten years of ministry on this mission field, the Christ-centered team of Angels were privileged to meet, feed, clothe, and pray for more than 7,000 victims of sex trafficking in just three areas of the city of Detroit. It was their honor to be chosen to share the love of Christ with each of them. The Lord led them as a united team to make over 600 rescues of His children from the streets. To God be all the glory!